JANICE
THOMPSON

Writing

PEACE

⋅ ON ⋅

My Heart

A 6-WEEK BIBLE
MEMORY DEVOTIONAL

BARBOUR
PUBLISHING

Published by Barbour Publishing, Inc., 1810 Barbour Drive, Uhrichsville, Ohio 44683, www.barbourbooks.com

Our mission is to inspire the world with the life-changing message of the Bible.

Member of the
Evangelical Christian
Publishers Association

Printed in China.

Week One:

PEACE TO OVERCOME TROUBLES

These things I have spoken unto you, that in me ye might have peace. In the world ye shall have tribulation: but be of good cheer; I have overcome the world.

JOHN 16:33

Week 1: DAY ONE
NOT WHY BUT HOW

Life can feel traumatizing at times. Between the nightly news, personal health crises, family woes, and friendship struggles, you might look at all that's swirling around you and say, "How am I supposed to feel peaceful in the middle of all of this?" It might be easier to squeeze your eyes shut, head to your bedroom, and crawl under the covers. At least there you're not faced with the craziness. You can hide away for a while.

Here's a hopeful promise from the Word of God: in Jesus, you can have peace no matter what you're facing. Whether it's a rough diagnosis from the doctor, betrayal from a spouse who's walking out the door, or upsetting news about one of your children, God will take care of you. Even when you're in the cold, stark reality of the pain, peace can flood your soul and guard your heart from the trauma. If you plant His Word deep in your heart, it will blossom and grow and give you everything you need to not only survive but thrive.

John 16:33 makes it clear that believers will face tribulation. There's no escaping it, hard as you might try. If you study the lives of believers from biblical days until now, you will see that many faced unbearable traumas—deaths of loved ones, critical illnesses, agonizing pain, intense suffering, and so on. Yet somehow these mighty men and women went on to do unimaginable things for the Lord.

He has amazing things for you to accomplish too. You'll come through the struggles stronger, healthier, and better equipped to serve others. In order for this to happen, you must make a critical choice in the midst of the battle. Instead of crying out, "Why, Lord?" incline your ear to Him and ask, "*How*, Lord? *How* will You lead me through this?" He has a plan to do just that, and it starts by learning, memorizing, and applying His Word then seeing the fruit. Through your work in the Bible, the Lord will teach you how to walk closely with Him not just in hard times but in good ones as well.

Believe it or not, the good and bad can happen simultaneously. We're encouraged in John 16:33 to "be of good cheer." When you think of "cheer," you usually think of a party or some sort of celebration. You don't usually place that word in the same sentence with "tribulation." Oh, but you can, and you should! Peace and trauma can dwell side by side, floating along seamlessly together.

Seem impossible? In the natural, it's not possible. The only way to truly understand the kind of peace Jesus offers is to accept that it's supernatural. It requires you to elevate your thinking above and beyond the realm of the natural. You can't possibly have peace in the midst of trauma unless it's poured down from heaven supernaturally.

Even now, in the middle of your chaos, Jesus is speaking: peace, peace, wonderful peace! Can you hear Him?

"The Lord bless you and keep you; the Lord make his face shine on you and be gracious to you; the Lord turn his face toward you and give you peace."
Numbers 6:24–26 niv

The Blank Page

You want peace in your life. . .lasting peace. You're done with the chaos and confusion. You've given yourself the big speech about how you're going to be more peaceful. You've memorized applicable verses from the Bible. But peace still seems to be a long way off, no matter how hard you work at it. Why?

Picture a gardener staring at a dry, crusty patch of land. He must somehow turn this barren place into an oasis fit for cabbages, cucumbers, and a host of other luscious vegetables. How does he manage the task? If he plants even the best seeds in that dry, broken soil, they won't stand a chance of flourishing.

Every good farmer knows that he must prepare the soil to ready it for the seeds he will plant. The same is true of the human heart. You could preach to yourself all day long. You could take ten million lovely seeds from the words of the Bible and attempt to plant them in your heart, but if you haven't taken adequate time to prepare your heart, those seeds will fall on dry ground.

Are you ready to submit to the King of kings and say, "Lord, have Your way in this hard, crusty heart"? Are you completely subjected to His authority not only in your life but in the circumstances swirling around you? Only when you've carefully examined the soil can you consider what will become of that garden.

The Last Word

Getting into the Word should be part of your daily routine. God wants you to dig deep, to discover new and exciting truths, and to apply them to your life so that your faith can grow, your joy can flourish, and the peace that only He can bring can reign.

Perhaps you say, "You don't understand. My life is nuts. If I had the time, I would totally do it; but I have kids, a house, laundry, a job. . .I just can't make that type of commitment."

Take a look at the great heroes of the faith—the men and women in Old and New Testament stories. Did they lead easy, carefree lives? Absolutely not! David had his Goliath (not to mention a lion and a bear). Daniel had a den full of hungry lions. Joseph had his pit. Job faced catastrophic, unexpected losses. Even Paul had his thorn in the flesh. Still, they all went on to do remarkable things for the Lord, and so can you!

There will always be distractions. There will always be excuses. But you can still dig into the Word and come away with nuggets of truth, even if your day doesn't allow for hours of study.

What if you make a commitment to wake up ten minutes earlier every morning to spend time in the Bible? If you do that every day for a year, you will have spent nearly sixty-one hours in the Word, discovering and applying great truths.

You can do it. No excuses!

Week 1: DAY TWO
PEACE WHEN YOU'RE MOVING IN GOD'S WILL

You've decided to lay down your excuses. You're going to get into the Word and apply it to your life. You're trusting the Lord to adequately prepare your heart so that you're ready for whatever He has in store for you throughout this journey toward lasting peace.

Awesome! Perhaps one of the first lessons God longs to teach you is this: it is possible to experience peace in the very middle of your turmoil if you're moving in His perfect will.

There's a remarkable story in the book of Acts that proves this point so beautifully. Paul the evangelist has just taken on a new traveling companion, a man named Silas. Together, they have traveled throughout many regions sharing the Gospel. They've established a church in Philippi, where God has done remarkable things. Talk about being in the center of God's will!

You know how it is though. Every time you're making strides for the kingdom of God, the enemy of your soul gets riled up. He just can't take it, so he kicks back. Such was the case here. Town leaders had Paul and Silas arrested, beaten, and thrown in prison, where their feet were placed in stocks.

No doubt you read that and think, "Okay, then. I'm out. If doing great things for the Lord means I'm going to end up in chains, you can forget it!"

Oh, but don't give up on the story just yet. Instead of panicking, Paul and Silas chose to sing and praise their way through the night. At midnight, a rumble stirred from the ground below. A massive earthquake hit the place with such force that it shattered the prisoners' chains and flung wide the prison doors. In just an instant, the entire situation changed all because these two godly men opened the door to a miracle by praising their God!

Instead of sprinting toward the nearest exit, Paul and Silas took time to connect with the jailer, who was terrified he would be blamed for the jail break. They shared the Gospel with this man, and before long, he and his entire household were saved. See what God can do if you don't panic in the middle of the trial?

There's tremendous power in not giving up when tribulations come, especially when you're following hard after God and moving according to His will. You can witness the same supernatural peace Paul and Silas experienced if you trust God through the trials and avoid saying, "But God! I was doing what You asked me to do. Why did this happen to me?"

By the way, Paul and Silas went on to do great things for God, and so will you. He has amazing plans for you.

Give thanks in all circumstances;
for this is the will of God in Christ Jesus for you.
1 THESSALONIANS 5:18 ESV

❧ The Blank Page ❧

God is using your life to paint many colorful stories. He has already penned many, but there are hundreds—if not thousands—yet to be written. He's an amazing author, writing word after hopeful word, and all with one purpose in mind: to show the world how much He loves them. Your life reflects that love, and your life stories can lead people on a journey toward the Savior if you will allow them to.

So, what stories are you hoping others will read? When they examine your life, will they see someone who—like Paul or Silas—praises her way through tough situations? Or will they see a frazzled, emotional woman who snaps at others when she faces trials and tribulations?

Today, take inventory. Make a list of the not-so-great things that have tainted the soil of your heart, making it harder to absorb the good seeds of God's Word. Perhaps you'll list things like bitterness, unforgiveness, jealousy, or a bad temper. Maybe you'll have to admit to harder things like sexual sin, lust, greed, or hatred. Dig deep. Make that list and hide nothing from the Lord.

You're not perfect, and that list proves it. But once you've examined the soil of your heart and have admitted there are areas that need tending, God can do the real work. Ask for His forgiveness and watch as He tends the soil and prepares you to receive true and lasting peace for the journey ahead.

❧ The Last Word ❧

You've discovered that God can bring peace in the middle of the trials you face as long as you're moving in His perfect will. You've admitted there are areas in the soil of your heart that need tending, and you're ready to let God do the deep work necessary. But you're still nervous inside. What if His heart-work is painful or difficult?

Consider the life of Richard Wurmbrand, a man of Jewish descent, who was born in Romania in the early 1900s. As an adult, he converted to Christianity and became a minister. Because he lived in a communist nation, he was not legally allowed to speak publicly about his faith. To do so could result in his death, but that didn't stop Richard. He faced persecution for his faith but survived and eventually founded Voice of the Martyrs, an international organization that defends the rights of persecuted Christians throughout the world. He's best known for his memoir, *Tortured for Christ*.

What if fear had shut Richard down? Thank goodness he didn't allow that! Because he went on to spread the Gospel, thousands of people came to Christ and are now experiencing true and lasting peace. Such are the possibilities if we submit ourselves to God's process and don't give up.

From now on a fire burned within us, as it did in the disciples on the road to Emmaus. "Snowflakes cannot fall on a hot stove," says an Indian proverb. The coldness of this world could no longer harm us, although we had to pass through bitter times.
—RICHARD WURMBRAND, *CHRIST ON THE JEWISH ROAD*

Week 1: DAY THREE
PEACE iN THE LiONS' DEN

The day started like any other. Daniel had no way of knowing it would end in a den of roaring lions. No doubt you've had days like that too. Oh, not days where you ended up face-to-face with feisty felines, but days that got off on the right foot and rapidly turned south. On those days, it's easy to let peace slip through the cracks and crevices of your heart, disappearing from view. But the Word of God makes it clear: you don't have to.

Let's take a closer look at how Daniel held on to his peace. His trial really began when his jealous rival, Darius, issued a decree that for thirty days no one in the kingdom could pray to any god or man except for Darius himself. The punishment for those who disobeyed? They would be condemned to death. Daniel ignored the decree and continued to pray to the one true God.

When the king heard what his good friend Daniel had done, he was heartbroken. How could he condemn a friend to death? However, not wanting to look spineless, the king had to follow the letter of the law. He had Daniel thrown into a den (or pit) filled with lions, hungry for the kill.

Daniel landed in front of the lions, and something crazy happened. They ignored him completely. Now, we don't know how it all went down because there's no video to watch, but if you study the habits of hungry lions, you know they don't shy away from a tasty meal. Daniel was their intended entrée, but God closed the mouths of the lions.

Wow! The Lord intervened in a miraculous way! He didn't

deliver Daniel from the pit. He didn't change the king's mind. Instead, right there, in the very middle of the storm, He simply closed the lions' mouths.

Chances are you're not facing a den of ravenous lions, but perhaps you are looking at a mountain of debt or a significant breakdown in your marriage, things that threaten your peace. You see those troubles coming at you like sharp-toothed lions, ready for the kill.

But God...

Oh, the joy of those two words! But God intervenes and provides the solution in the simplest of ways. And when that happens, all of your worries just float away. The Lord interrupts your impossible with His possible.

There's more to Daniel's story. When the king realized God had intervened, his thinking became crystal clear. In that moment, when he saw what the Lord had done, the king turned the tables. Before long, Darius faced those hungry lions, only this time there was no supernatural deliverance.

You want to know how to live above your circumstances, how to find peace and joy in the midst of trials? Saturate yourself in stories like this. Don't just read them...absorb them. In doing so, you'll see that God is and always has been a deliverer of those who diligently seek Him.

May the God of peace be with you all. Amen.
ROMANS 15:33 ESV

The Blank Page

The Word of God is like bread that we should hunger for. In Matthew 4:4 (NIV), Jesus says, "Man shall not live on bread alone, but on every word that comes from the mouth of God." So, we are to sincerely desire the Word of God as one would come before a meal with an empty stomach.

Think back to those lions in Daniel's story. They were deliberately starved before their victims were thrown into the pit. They weren't just hungry. They were, as modern-day teens might say, "hangry." Ravenous. Starving. Nothing but God's miraculous intervention could stop them from consuming their prey. Their nature propelled them to kill and eat.

Now, if you've ever been really, *really* hungry and smelled a juicy steak cooking, you have some clue what that's like. That sizzling hunk of meat is your prey, and nothing can stop you from diving in.

God wants you to have that same desire for His Word. He wants you to come to it, spiritual stomach rumbling, ready to be filled. That's why He's so keen on getting the soil of your heart ready: because He knows all that's waiting for you once you're ready to receive.

Are you hungry for His Word today? If not, perhaps there's something holding you back. Spend some time praying, and ask God if there are areas of your heart that still need addressing. Once you've allowed Him to prepare you for the feast He's offered in His Word, you'll be ready to consume His Word as never before.

❧ The Last Word ❧

If you've studied church history, you know that many powerful evangelists abandoned all to spread the Gospel during what has become known as "the Great Awakening" period. An inner fire unlike anything experienced in prior generations drove those godly men and women to preach, to share, and to convert people to Christ. No one had to say, "Hey, why don't you go tell someone about Jesus?" These fired-up believers couldn't sleep, eat, or breathe until they shared the joy of the Gospel message with everyone they met along the way.

The same inner passion that fueled men like Jonathan Edwards, George Whitfield, and the Wesley brothers is burning inside of you even now. Oh, it might be just a tiny spark at the moment, but if you fan it, it will grow into a fierce flame that can catch your world on fire.

Developing a passion for God's Word is where it starts. To know Him, you must know His Word. And once you get that Word in your heart, it takes root and gives you a passion for people. Once that starts, watch out! Your passion will become contagious!

Perhaps Jonathan Edwards put it best when he said, "God's purpose for my life was that I have a passion for God's glory and that I have a passion for my joy in that glory, and that these two are one passion."

How is your passion today, friend? Perhaps it's time to fan that ember into a powerful flame.

Week 1: DAY FOUR
PEACE ON THE BATTLEFIELD

"This isn't a battle I ever thought I'd have to fight." How many times have you used those words? Isn't it interesting how you can be moving along, everything going well, and then...*bam!* Up pops a giant. You stare at him, shocked that he's somehow appeared from out of nowhere, and then you freeze in place. Fear slips in, and before you know it, your peace is gone. All you can see is that massive problem, looming in front of you.

Here's some excellent news: God never intended for the giants to rob you of your peace. Even when you're facing news of Goliath proportions, you can still sense the overwhelming, supernatural presence of your heavenly Father as He cocoons you in His peace.

Still not sure? Check out the story of David. On the day Goliath (a nine-foot giant) tried to take him down, the young shepherd boy wasn't having it. Instead of allowing his enemy to rob him of his peace, David was filled with the boldness of God. He blurted out the words, "You come against me with sword and spear and javelin, but I come against you in the name of the LORD Almighty, the God of the armies of Israel, whom you have defied" (1 Samuel 17:45 NIV).

Well, now. That changes everything! When you realize you have the backing (and the power) of the Creator of the universe, no enemy can rise against you.

Clearly, no one had to convince David of this. He continued to give that giant a piece of his mind:

> *"This day the LORD will deliver you into my hands, and I'll strike you down and cut off your head. This very day I will give the carcasses of the Philistine army to the birds and the wild animals, and the whole world will know that there is a God in Israel. All those gathered here will know that it is not by sword or spear that the LORD saves; for the battle is the LORD's, and he will give all of you into our hands."*
>
> 1 SAMUEL 17:46–47 NIV

Don't you love David's boldness and tenacity? His courage came from a place of deep conviction. He recognized what we often do not—the battle isn't ours. It is God's.

Sure, you get scared from time to time. And yes, the enemy does his level best to rob you of your peace, but then you remember: "Wait a minute! This is in *His* hands, not mine." In that very moment, as the realization sets in, your peace returns along with a boldness that propels you forward!

Give this week's memory verse (John 16:33) a closer look. In this world, you *will* have tribulation. However, Jesus spoke the words: "But be of good cheer; I have overcome the world." Why did He share that particular message with His followers? The answer is found in the first part of the verse: "These things I have spoken unto you, that in me ye might have peace."

He knew you would need it, friend, and He has already made provision.

> *The LORD gives strength to his people;*
> *the LORD blesses his people with peace.*
>
> PSALM 29:11 NIV

The Blank Page

The gardener stares at the unusable soil, ponders his plan, and then reaches into his bag of tricks. He chooses compost, organic matter made from broken-down plant material, to replenish the nutrients and to make that soil rich and hearty once again. With great care, he spreads it over the soil, covering every square inch.

In much the same way, God tends to your heart. He supernaturally infuses you with spiritual nutrients to make that soil usable and pliable once more. The Lord's compost provides a cover—a shelter if you will. Psalm 91:4 (NIV) puts it like this: "He will cover you with his feathers, and under his wings you will find refuge; his faithfulness will be your shield and rampart."

Nothing is left exposed when Jesus tends to your heart. He covers it all to prevent any further damage while bringing healing to your mind, will, and emotions. No matter what you've been through in the past, no matter how deep the hurts or wounds, you can still be ready to receive His Word if you allow Him to cover and nurture you.

And what joy when that happens! When your heart is ready, you can look at verses like John 16:33 and see them as living, breathing, active possibilities in your life. They're not just words on a page anymore. They're life-changing, Spirit-infused promises from the heart of a Father-Gardener who adores you more than you can imagine.

The Last Word

Sometimes the giants we face are so powerful, so huge, that they seem unstoppable. No matter how hard you fight, they continue to torment you. Christians who've suffered persecution at the hands of oppressive governments would probably nod in agreement, for they understand better than most. Regimes that stand in opposition to God aren't an easy takedown even when you have David-like faith.

Perhaps it's time to admit that the Lord can use even the worst opponent for our good. He can take an unfair worldly system that the enemy pits against us and use it to deepen our faith and strengthen our walk with Him. He can plant peace deep in our hearts even if Goliath doesn't fall when we throw those stones.

Brother Yun, a house church leader in China who faced multiple years of persecution, said it best: "The world can do nothing to a Christian who has no fear of man" (Brother Yun, *The Heavenly Man*). When you truly live like that, even the most powerful regime has no hold on you.

Who—or what—do you fear today? What giants loom large? What forces seem too great? List those things on a page then offer them up to God. He will battle on your behalf if you truly allow Him. Breathe in the words "I have overcome the world." He has, you know. As you memorize those words, let them bring life and hope. In Him, you are an overcomer.

Week 1: DAY FIVE
PEACE IN THE FIERY TRIALS

If you've lived for more than, say, a day, you've probably experienced fiery trials. (Definition: fiery trial = regular trial x 100.) When those situations rise, they can be shocking, terrifying, and even life-threatening. Having God's Word buried deep in your heart can save you from distress as you maneuver your way through those unexpected, heart-pounding events.

No one understood fiery trials more than the three Hebrew youths—Shadrach, Meshach, and Abednego. These young men refused to bow down to the king, their loyalty remaining steadfast to God instead. The price for their high crime? They were tossed into a fiery furnace.

Most of us would do anything to avoid walking into a burning building. The goal is avoiding fire, not running toward it. But these fellows were willing to give their lives, if necessary, to remain faithful to God. Check out the boldness of this trio:

Shadrach, Meshach and Abednego replied to him,
"King Nebuchadnezzar, we do not need to defend
ourselves before you in this matter. If we are thrown into
the blazing furnace, the God we serve is able to deliver
us from it, and he will deliver us from Your Majesty's
hand. But even if he does not, we want you to know,
Your Majesty, that we will not serve your gods or
worship the image of gold you have set up."
DANIEL 3:16–18 NIV

Whoa. Pause to think about their reaction for a moment. "Even if he does not, we want you to know. . ." Who has that kind of boldness? A child of God who is saturated in the Word and empowered by the Spirit, that's who! When you're filled to overflowing with the confidence that only God can give, you can face the flames without losing your cool.

No doubt you know how the story ends. Not only are the lives of Shadrach, Meshach, and Abednego spared, but they are joined in the fire by a visitor!

"Look!" Nebuchadnezzar said. "I see four men, unbound, walking around in the fire unharmed! And the fourth looks like a god!" (Daniel 3:25 NLT).

Was it Jesus? An angel? Opinions vary, but one thing is undeniable: they were not alone.

You're not alone, either. Begin to memorize verses like Deuteronomy 31:8 (NIV): "The LORD himself goes before you and will be with you; he will never leave you nor forsake you. Do not be afraid; do not be discouraged." When those words become more than words to you, nothing can rob you of your peace, not even the fieriest of trials.

"When you pass through the waters, I will be with you;
and through the rivers, they shall not overwhelm you;
when you walk through fire you shall not be burned,
and the flame shall not consume you."
ISAIAH 43:2 ESV

The Blank Page

Ask yourself this question: "Have I grown as a result of the fiery trials I've walked through?"

No doubt your faith has quadrupled, your resolve strengthened, and your testimony blossomed. God is hard at work, developing you into someone who can impact the world for Jesus. Kudos on not allowing the pain to harden the soil of your heart. On the contrary, you've asked the Lord to use the difficult circumstances to enrich the soil so that you might take His Word and hide it in your heart.

If you study a farmer's methods, you'll see that he often uses bone meal, a type of fertilizer made of animal bones. It's a finely ground powder added to the soil to supply phosphorus.

You might read that and think, "Man, that's awful. Animals had to die so the soil could be strengthened?" Here's a hard truth: some of the fiery trials you walk through will feel like death to you. But remember this promise from the Word of God: "And we know that for those who love God all things work together for good, for those who are called according to his purpose" (Romans 8:28 ESV).

No pain is wasted. God grinds it to a fine powder and applies it to your heart so that you are able to absorb the truth of His Word. Why? To experience supernatural peace in the midst of it all.

The Last Word

Horatio clutched the railing of the ship's lower deck, overlooking the mighty Atlantic. When he pinched his eyes shut, he could see the faces of his four children—Annie, Maggie, Bessie, and Tanetta—who had perished at sea aboard the SS *Ville du Havre* weeks prior.

Monstrous waves lapped at the boat as the ship hovered over the very spot where his precious little ones had lost their lives. And though his heart was broken into a million pieces, Horatio's first words were not "Why, God?" Instead, from a place of complete peace, he penned the lyrics that have now been sung in thousands of churches across the globe:

> *When peace like a river attendeth my way,*
> *when sorrows like sea billows roll,*
> *Whatever my lot, Thou hast taught me to say:*
> *It is well, it is well with my soul.*
> HORATIO SPAFFORD, "IT IS WELL WITH MY SOUL"

It's impossible to fathom such a loss, let alone such a brave, peace-filled response. But the "How did he do it?" question is answered in a later verse of the song:

> *For me, be it Christ, be it Christ hence to live:*
> *If Jordan above me shall roll,*
> *No pain shall be mine, for in death as in life*
> *Thou wilt whisper Thy peace to my soul.*

The Lord took what the enemy meant for evil and used it for good in Horatio's life. He ground the pain into a fine powder and applied it like a salve. The Author of all whispered "Peace, be still" to Horatio's heart, and He will do no less for you, no matter what fiery trials you're facing today.

Week 1: DAY SIX
PEACE WHEN YOU'RE CALLED TO SACRIFICE

You've made great strides in your walk toward a peace-filled life. You've allowed God to deal with the hardened areas of your heart, and you are learning that pain and peace often ride side by side on this life journey. You've been asked to make sacrifices along the way, and some of them have been painful. You still secretly wonder why things are so tough.

There's a sobering story in the seventh chapter of Acts about a young man named Stephen who was martyred for the cause of Christ. The most remarkable thing happened as his accusers stood before him with stones in their hands, ready to end his life and his ministry. Stephen, full of the Holy Spirit, looked up to heaven and said, "Look! I see the heavens opened and the Son of Man standing at the right hand of God!" (Acts 7:56 NKJV).

This made his accusers even angrier. They began to rant and scream at the top of their lungs. Then they rushed him, dragged him out of the city, and began stoning him. You would think this would be the end of Stephen's peaceful response, but the scripture teaches us otherwise: "While they were stoning him, Stephen prayed, 'Lord Jesus, receive my spirit.' Then he fell on his knees and cried out, 'Lord, do not hold this sin against them.' When he had said this, he fell asleep" (Acts 7:59–60 NIV).

Wow. What sort of spiritual powerhouse would you have to be to forgive your perpetrators even as they were stoning you to death? Yet somehow the Spirit of God so consumed Stephen that he didn't see them as his attackers but rather as men in need of Christ's love.

Stephen was called by God to make the ultimate sacrifice: to give his life for the cause of Christ. Chances are very good you won't be called upon to make that same sacrifice, but perhaps there will be things the Lord asks you to lay down: unhealthy relationships, that home you always wanted but can't really afford, even (on occasion) a job opportunity or financial gain. It's never easy to lay something down, and many people struggle with anger at God during sacrificial seasons.

Maybe we should, as the writer of Hebrews suggests, "continually offer to God a sacrifice of praise—the fruit of lips that openly profess his name" (Hebrews 13:15 NIV). We can live like that only when we have a supernatural understanding that everything we have is His—our possessions, our jobs, our relationships, our time, even our very lives. If we agree to hold nothing back, we will never feel like anything has been taken from us. Oh, the peace we will experience by simply letting go.

I appeal to you therefore, brothers, by the mercies of God, to present your bodies as a living sacrifice, holy and acceptable to God, which is your spiritual worship.
ROMANS 12:1 ESV

The Blank Page

Experts say it takes twenty-one days to form a habit. You're trying to get into the habit of reading and memorizing scripture so that your faith can be strengthened and your peace deeply planted. But you're not sure you can stick with it for one day, let alone twenty-one. You have about ten thousand other things to do each day, after all, and most of those are set in stone. Sure, a few could be tossed aside, but doing so might call for sacrifice, and no one likes that.

Consider this truth from bestselling author and speaker John Maxwell: "You'll never change your life until you change something you do daily. The secret of your success is found in your daily routine."

The only way to truly change your habits is to change your habits. (Sounds simple, doesn't it?) But how? Laying down the old and picking up the new requires work, and you're already so busy.

When the gardener preps the soil for planting, he aerates it. The process of aeration breaks it up and leaves air pockets that promote better water drainage. These air pockets give the incoming plants a better chance of settling in and growing.

God wants air pockets in your daily schedule. Right now, He's having to compete with so many other things. Some of them are really good things—family, friends, job, and so on. But the others? Not so much.

What will it take for you to create space for Him today? Is giving up something you enjoy in order to spend more time with the Savior worth the sacrifice?

The Last Word

The word *sacrifice* is defined as the "destruction or surrender of something for the sake of something else" (Merriam-Webster).

Pause to think about that for a moment. When you sacrifice something you care about (say, your favorite cake or cookies), you're doing so for the sake of something else (a trimmer physique and lower blood sugar). Every sacrifice is loaded with potential for something greater. If you can begin to see your sacrifices through this filter before the "laying down" process, you will be able to release them with inexplicable peace in your heart. Why? Because you know something greater is coming.

Ponder the sacrifice of Jesus on the cross. If you had witnessed it firsthand, the shock and horror of it all might have wrecked you. Likely, you wouldn't have been able to see past the pain and agony to the beauty on the other side of His sacrifice. Aren't you glad He could see and was willing to carry through so that you could have eternal life?

Sacrifice (in the moment) brings pain. There's no denying it. But when its potential is fully realized, it brings nothing but peace and joy. And there's nothing better than having the assurance from His Word that things really will get better: "And the peace of God, which surpasses all understanding, will guard your hearts and your minds in Christ Jesus" (Philippians 4:7 ESV).

What is God asking you to lay down today for the sake of something else?

Week 1: DAY SEVEN
PEACE TO OVERCOME

There's an African proverb that goes something like this: "Smooth seas do not make skillful sailors." That's a hard truth, isn't it? So many times, we look at the rough seas and cry out, "Lord, just take it away! Make it stop." But He looks back with a smile and says, "Oh, but I'm growing you into someone of great strength. Don't stop now!"

You are an overcomer. You've made it through so many hard times, and you'll continue to grow in strength as you submit your will to His. As you study His Word, as those scriptures come alive in your heart, you'll begin to see yourself differently. Instead of looking at troubles and saying, "I can't!" you'll begin to say, "He can." It's all about His work, you know, not your own.

Think about the work Jesus accomplished on the cross. When He took your sin upon Himself, He accomplished salvation (eternal life) for you and for all who would believe and receive Him. And when He rose again three days later, He conquered sin and death. Jesus overcame even the most formidable obstacle—the grave—and did it with you in mind.

Take a look at this week's memory verse in a different version: "I have said these things to you, that in me you may have peace. In the world you will have tribulation. But take heart; I have overcome the world" (John 16:33 ESV).

When Jesus said, "I have overcome the world," He wasn't just talking about His own personal journey. His words were for you as well. Why else would He have made such a specific promise after mentioning the tribulations you would go through? He overcame the enemy of your soul when He conquered death, and because He took the enemy down, you can have victory over your tribulations. All He asks is that you begin to see yourself as a victor not because of your own works but because of His.

Because of what Jesus has accomplished, you can live as an overcomer, filled with the supernatural peace spoken about in John 16:33. Psalm 118:15 (NIV) confirms this: "Shouts of joy and victory resound in the tents of the righteous: 'The LORD's right hand has done mighty things!' "

There's a role for you to play too. You have to change your perspective to begin to see yourself as a victor! Ask Him to give you a sense of expectation as you come to His Word. As you read and absorb the scriptures, anticipate growth. Expect peace to flood your soul and His Word to come alive in your heart, even in the middle of the battle.

For everyone who has been born of God overcomes the world. And this is the victory that has overcome the world— our faith. Who is it that overcomes the world except the one who believes that Jesus is the Son of God?

1 JOHN 5:4–5 ESV

The Blank Page

There's a gardening term that farmers are familiar with: _tilth_. This term describes the health of the soil. When the gardener takes everything into consideration—the pH levels, nutrient balance, water, and air—he determines the overall quality and readiness of the soil. If all those things are as they should be, he says the soil is in good tilth.

Is the soil of your heart in good tilth? Are you ready to begin reading and absorbing the Word of God? If so, dive on in! But remember, the farmer never stops checking the soil's quality, even after those seeds are planted. It's a never-ending journey to keep it healthy at every step of the way.

Oh, the seeds God wants to grow in your heart as you take this journey toward peace! The words in your Bible are so much more than mere words! They are the very thoughts of God. When you memorize them, when they become ingrained in you, speaking them over your situations comes naturally. In the middle of a crisis, you will cry out: "God, You've spoken it over me! You've told me in Your Word that I can have peace and that I can be of good cheer in spite of my tribulations. I can do all these things because of You, Lord! You have overcome the world, so I am a victor in Your name!"

When those are the first words that spring to your lips in a crisis, you can truly say that the soil of your heart is in good tilth.

The Last Word

In January 1956, the entire world changed for Elisabeth Elliot. Her husband, Jim, left their missionary headquarters in Quito, Ecuador, along with several other team members. Their goal? To contact the unreached Auca (Huaorani) tribe so that they could share the Gospel message with the people there. Unfortunately, Jim and the other missionaries were speared down by tribal natives, and all five lost their lives.

Though devastated, Elisabeth continued her work with a different tribe (the Quechua). Through a series of miraculous events, she was eventually invited to live among the Huaoranis—the very people who had killed her husband. Elisabeth was instrumental in leading many of them to the Lord, including the man responsible for Jim's death.

As you read this story, can you picture yourself in Elisabeth's shoes? Can you imagine taking your two young children and living among the people who had taken the one person you most cared about? It seems impossible, doesn't it? Yet Elisabeth was led by peace as she took those steps into the jungle to do God's work. She was truly a victor over her circumstances!

Over the past few days, we've discussed the word *sacrifice*. We've talked about the *tilth* of our heart and the need for usability. We've discussed the truth that God wants us to absorb His Word so that it becomes a living, breathing part of us; and we've established that, through Jesus, we are overcomers. Elisabeth's story is proof that tribulations will come, but through His Spirit, you can rise above them and live in supernatural peace.

Week Two:

STRENGTH-GIVING PEACE

The LORD will give strength unto his people; the LORD will bless his people with peace.

PSALM 29:11

Week 2: DAY ONE
PEACE WHEN LIFE IS STRESSFUL

You've decided to start a new at-home exercise regime. The first day, you begin your workout with great enthusiasm. Three minutes in, and you're sweating. There's no way you're going to make it. Seven minutes in, and you're convinced you weren't made for this.

On the second day, your calves feel like they're on fire, but you decide to keep going. You make it to the fifteen-minute mark and collapse on the sofa. The following morning, you wake up feeling like you were run over by a truck. Still, your determination is greater than your pain, so you don't give up.

Over a period of days, things that once felt impossible become doable. You can work out longer, stretch farther, even lunge lower. . .all because you didn't give up. Muscles, tendons, ligaments. . .they're all getting stronger the more stress you place on them.

What's happening is a process called *eustress*. The more stress you put on those muscles, the stronger they get. The same is true when it comes to digging into the Word of God. The first day, perhaps, you can't stay focused. The second day, you're convinced this isn't going to work. But the longer you go, the longer you can go. And the deeper you dig, the deeper you can dig. When you reach the point where you begin to unearth treasures—verses like "The LORD will give strength unto his people; the LORD will bless his people with peace"—the more you realize the truth: you were made for this. You're placing stress on those spiritual muscles, and they're responding by getting stronger.

You're not the only one to gain strength during seasons of stress. Think of your favorite Bible characters. They allowed the eustress to make them stronger from the inside out.

Think of Mary, the mother of Jesus. Boy, did she ever have to find strength for her journey. And what about Joseph as he received the news of his bride-to-be's condition? If these two were alive in the twenty-first century, they'd be the focus of a reality show, and millions would be convinced their marriage wouldn't make it. But Mary found peace for the journey, as evidenced in her words: "My soul glorifies the Lord and my spirit rejoices in God my Savior, for he has been mindful of the humble state of his servant. From now on all generations will call me blessed, for the Mighty One has done great things for me—holy is his name" (Luke 1:46–49 NIV).

The world will call you blessed too, for you will be seen as a person of great strength as you turn your focus to the Word of God and to His glorious plan for your life despite the stresses.

Do not be anxious about anything, but in everything by prayer and supplication with thanksgiving let your requests be made known to God. And the peace of God, which surpasses all understanding, will guard your hearts and your minds in Christ Jesus.

PHILIPPIANS 4:6–7 ESV

❧ The Blank Page ❧

Stresses can harden you if you're not careful, and it's difficult to bring growth from a hardened shell. This makes Bible memorization particularly difficult. But here's some great news: <u>God has taken extra measures to soften you and prepare you for the road ahead, to bring down the walls you've built from your pain.</u> He's getting you ready for bigger, better things by knocking those walls down and tending to the deep places in your heart through His Word so that you can continue to grow in Him.

Picture the gardener looking over his flower seeds before planting them. Most can simply be scattered on bare dirt, but there are a few varieties that have tough seed coats. Sweet pea, nasturtium, milkweed, and morning glory are just a few examples of seeds with hardened shells. These tough seed coats were designed by God to keep them from accidentally sprouting too soon; but when the time is right, they need a little extra help.

How does the farmer prepare them for planting? He scars them (basically, scrapes and/or scratches them) and then soaks them in water. Sounds painful, right? Still, the payoff is terrific! They soften up slowly and are eventually ready for planting, all in the right season.

<u>God's softening process is a bit like the scarification process. It can be painful to allow Him to work on your heart during stressful seasons, but He uses every scar to make you more pliable in His hands.</u> Oh, what peace you can enjoy when you allow Him to scarify your heart.

The Last Word

Repeat these words: "Stress is my friend. Stress is my friend."

It might be difficult to comprehend the truth of those words, but when you allow the stresses of life to grow your spiritual muscles and when you allow God to scarify your heart in the process, eustress really can help you develop into a spiritual powerhouse. The key is to remain steadfast in your time with Him and in His Word. Otherwise, you will grow hard, like that morning glory seed.

Focus on verses like Isaiah 26:3 (NIV): "You will keep in perfect peace those whose minds are steadfast, because they trust in you." This is the formula used by generations of spiritual powerhouses, people who overcame great odds and who used eustress to propel them forward.

Think about that! When we get to heaven, we're going to meet thousands upon thousands of great men and women who lived their lives this way. We will hear their testimonies and admire their faith not because they were physically strong but because they overcame seemingly impossible situations and didn't allow the stresses to defeat them.

He will do the same for you too. And because He's God and delights in the impossible, He will write peace on your heart in the process.

> *Adopting the right attitude can convert*
> *a negative stress into a positive one.*
> —HANS SELYE

Week 2: DAY TWO
PEACE WHILE BELIEVING FOR THE IMPOSSIBLE

Perhaps you look at this week's Bible memory verse and think it sounds too good to be true. Does the Creator of the universe really see all you're going through? If so, will He really give you, His child, the strength you need to see your journey through to the end, flooding you with peace along the way. . .even if what you're facing seems impossible?

The answer to all of those questions is a resounding "Yes!" God has promised in His Word that He not only sees but also cares. He wants to use His Word to strengthen you so that you can go on to do great things.

Think of a parent with a young child just learning to walk. It's breaking Mom's heart to see her little one take tumble after tumble, falling over and over. It would be easier for her to pick the child up and carry her, but if she continued to do that, her little one would never learn. Instead, Mom gives her bucket-loads of encouragement as she makes attempt after attempt until, at last, she can toddle across the room, all giggles and smiles.

That's how God works in your life. He wants to strengthen your spiritual muscles in much the same way a toddler's leg muscles are strengthened as she learns to walk. Sure, your heavenly Father could rescue you from every tough situation, but would your muscles grow? Would the necessary eustress take place?

Why do you suppose the Lord cares so much about making you strong internally? To increase your faith, of course, and to help you believe for the impossible.

Consider the story of Hannah. For years, she waited, prayed, and believed for a child. She faced taunts from her oppressors and even ridicule from the local priest, who accused her of being drunk when she was simply praying and mourning. Talk about a rough road.

Still, she took those taunts and antagonistic words and used them to grow her spiritual muscles. As those muscles grew, so did her faith. God honored that faith and gave her a son, Samuel, who went on to do amazing things for the kingdom of God.

That's what happens when you learn to toddle, spiritually speaking. You fall down, you get back up again. When you do, you're stronger than ever, ready to do great things for the Lord. You're also more determined to see impossible situations turned around in Jesus' name!

The godly may trip seven times, but they will get up again.
But one disaster is enough to overthrow the wicked.
PROVERBS 24:16 NLT

The Blank Page

The farmer is very selective with his seeds. He wants to make sure they're hearty, sturdy, and disease-resistant. Start with a healthy seed, and you grow a healthy plant. Start with a poor seed, and it's more vulnerable to the attacks of the enemy (fungal, bacterial, or viral diseases; insects; and so on).

The same can be said of your journey as you memorize and apply the Word of God. Every bite of the Word of God is nutrient-packed and will make you hearty, sturdy, and able to resist the enemy's schemes. So, when you consume it daily, you're getting a megadose of spiritual vitamins. You're not as vulnerable to attack when you've planted the Word deep in your heart.

So, how do you go about memorizing verses? Here are a few suggestions that might prove helpful:

* *Sing them! Set the verses to music and then sing them to yourself daily.*
* *Write them down multiple times in a row.*
* *Put them on sticky notes around the house (for example, on the bathroom mirror).*
* *Create hand movements/motions for the various words of the verse.*
* *Use flash cards.*
* *Use a Bible memory app. (You'll find several available on your mobile device.)*

No matter how you go about it, memorization can be fun. And remember, as you consume those scriptures, you're planting healthy seeds so that you can grow stronger and more resistant to the plans of the enemy.

The Last Word

In 1961, a nineteen-year-old missionary named Bruce Olson made a decision that would forever change his life. Following the prompting of the Holy Spirit, he bought a one-way ticket to Colombia, his heart set on evangelizing unreached people.

His story is a harrowing one. While ministering to the Motilone tribe, he was captured by a band of guerrilla terrorists who were intent upon controlling Motilone territory.

Bruce (known to the natives as Bruchko) experienced horrors we could never imagine during his nine-month captivity. In the end, guerrilla leaders released him, claiming they had made a mistake in capturing him. (Can you imagine?) They saw the Spirit of God in this young man and knew they were messing with the wrong guy!

The repentant guerrillas agreed to leave the Motilone people alone, and Bruchko went back to his work, ministering to the lost. Many of the guerrillas, as well as tribal peoples, and others around the world who heard Bruchko's amazing testimony were won to the Lord. God used what the enemy meant for evil to reach untold masses!

Bruce Olson went into this adventure a spiritual toddler, barely walking. But his spiritual muscles grew as he faced opposition until, at last, he walked with confidence in all that God had planned for him.

The Lord has amazing adventures planned for you too! So, don't worry if you take a tumble or two. Get back up, dust yourself off, and keep on walking.

Week 2: DAY THREE
PEACE WHILE TURNING AROUND

Maybe you've heard (or used) the expression "Looks like I'd better do a one-eighty." That's an easy way to say "It's time to turn around and go the other way."

You've been there: you're hot and heavy into a situation and realize you've made some wrong choices. They've led you to a place you really don't need to be. The only way out is to turn around and go the other way. It's not easy, but if you keep plowing forward in the wrong direction, things are only going to get worse.

Here's a key illustration from scripture. Jonah, an Old Testament prophet, was summoned by God to go to Nineveh and confront the people about their sin problem. Jonah's response? "Um, nope. Don't think so." So, he took off in the opposite direction, headed for Joppa, where he jumped on board a ship that would take him far, far away.

Likely you've been in a similar position: God nudged you toward something difficult, and you didn't want to face it, so you tucked yourself away, hoping He wouldn't find you.

God found Jonah on board a ship headed to Tarshish. Through a series of cinema-worthy events, Jonah ends up getting tossed overboard and swallowed by a whale. (Hollywood could never do this story justice, could they?) Jonah survived but found himself trapped inside that great sea creature with plenty of time on his hands to think. . .and repent.

The whale coughed him up, and Jonah did what he should have done in the beginning—he went to Nineveh to preach to the people there. In other words, he did a one-eighty. The result? The people of Nineveh repented.

You might wonder what all of this has to do with this week's memory verse. As you've learned from Psalm 29:11, the Lord gives strength to His people and blesses them with peace. But sometimes we deliberately disobey and, in doing so, stop His hand of blessing. We can't receive all that He has for us when we're running in the opposite direction, and we sure don't have peace!

Stop to examine your life for a moment. Have you wondered why God seems to be blessing others with peace but not you? Is there any chance you've been running from Him in some area of your life? Take the time to pray that through, and see if He doesn't reveal some hidden spot where you've held on to rebellion.

It's never too late to do a one-eighty. Like Jonah, you can finally—even after a season of running—have total peace once again.

I will run in the way of your commandments
when you enlarge my heart!
PSALM 119:32 ESV

The Blank Page

If you've ever planted a garden, you're probably familiar with perennials. They are plants that return year after year of their own accord. You don't have to replant them each season. After hibernating for months on end, they simply sprout up on their own when the time is right. The potential was just underneath the surface the whole time.

When you memorize scriptures, you plant key verses deep in your heart. When the situation calls for it, even if you don't have a Bible in hand, those biblical truths come sprouting forth. Like those perennials, the potential was buried deep within you months (or even years) prior, when you decided to plant that seed-verse.

If you're going through a tough time, verses like John 14:27 (NLT) can spring to mind with no effort at all: "I am leaving you with a gift—peace of mind and heart. And the peace I give is a gift the world cannot give. So don't be troubled or afraid."

Want to live this way? Walk in obedience to God. Go where He calls you to go. Do what He calls you to do. Repent when you need to repent. And, along the way, dig deep in the Bible for truths you can bury in your heart. When you least expect it (but most need it), those hidden truths will crack the surface of the nutrient-rich soil and be released into the stratosphere, where they will change your life for the better.

✿ The Last Word ✿

Maybe you're in a place you never planned to be. You've painted yourself into a proverbial corner or caused some sort of upheaval or unrest in your walk with God. It's not too late. You can always do a one-eighty.

Such was the case with a young man named Nicky Cruz. Born in Puerto Rico, Cruz moved to New York at the age of fifteen and joined the Mau Mau street gang. He was named warlord of the gang shortly thereafter and soon became their president.

You would think a man like this would be lost forever, wouldn't you? But a street preacher, David Wilkerson, approached Cruz and spoke the words, "Jesus loves you and will never stop loving you." Cruz got so angry, he hit David and threatened to kill him.

It took a lot of patience on Wilkerson's part, but Cruz eventually attended an evangelistic meeting and began to feel remorse for the things he had done. He responded to the altar call, and his life was forever changed.

Cruz went on to become a Christian evangelist and led many to the Lord. Wow, talk about doing a one-eighty! Maybe you've read his testimony in *The Cross and the Switchblade.*

This story brings such hope, doesn't it? Perhaps you still need to turn some areas of your life around. It's not too late. Or maybe there are those in your inner circle who are running from God. You've prayed, you've believed, and now you're not sure what to do. Stand on this week's scripture. God will fill you with strength and give you supernatural peace even while you wait.

Week 2: DAY FOUR
PEACE WHEN THE WALLS ARE TUMBLING

Sometimes the enemies we face are so formidable we feel completely dwarfed by them. They loom before us like fortified cities, and we can't imagine how or if we'll ever penetrate their walls.

Picture Joshua, approaching the walls of Jericho. Despite God's promise that he would take the city, he had to somehow get past those walls first. No doubt he stood at a distance, stared at them, and said, "Um, nope. I don't think so."

Maybe you can relate. You've been called to something big, but you keep running into brick walls. You huff and puff (just like the three little pigs), but you simply can't blow those walls down. And they're not budging. They're just as big an obstacle now as when you started your journey, and your strength is waning.

God commanded Joshua and his men to march around the city of Jericho for seven days in a row. On the first six days, they were told to march around the town once per day, carrying the ark of the covenant and blowing their horns. (Talk about announcing your arrival!) On the seventh day, they were instructed to march around the city seven times and then let out a shout. When that final triumphant moment came, Joshua hollered out, "Shout! For the LORD has given you the town!" (Joshua 6:16 NLT). The people responded with a shout that must've sent shivers down the spines of the people inside that walled fortress.

Imagine God asking you to march around your proverbial Jericho. Maybe a mountain of debt or a medical problem. Can you see yourself garnering the strength and faith to keep going around and around until at last the walls come tumbling down? (Side note: it takes God less than a millisecond to knock down walls that it might take us years to destroy. Just one breath from the Holy Spirit and walls have to come down!)

What "walled city" are you facing today? What's robbing you of your peace and keeping you from experiencing true freedom? If you want to see those walls fall down, start by acknowledging that you can't do it on your own. Then be prepared to do it God's way even if His way seems nonsensical. He might ask you to give money away—to your church, ministry, or missionary—while you're fretting over not having enough. Sometimes His methods can seem a bit different from our own, but remember, He's working everything together for your good. To have ultimate peace, you must learn to trust Him even before those walls fall down. So, what are you waiting for? Start marching!

The seventh time around, as the priests sounded the long blast on their horns, Joshua commanded the people, "Shout! For the Lord has given you the town!"
JOSHUA 6:16 NLT

The Blank Page

By their very nature, walls separate and divide. They keep one group from another. The walls you erect in your heart can separate you from loved ones, but they can also separate you from God if you let them. And when you have those proverbial walls firmly in place, your time in the Word can seem pretty pointless. Words—even God-breathed ones—don't stick to walls of unforgiveness and pain after all.

Today, as you approach the Word of God, ask the Lord a question: "What is my Jericho? Are there any walls that need to come down so that I can have total victory in my faith life with nothing held back?" Perhaps you've been blocking unwanted feelings or hiding from God or others in some way. If so, ask for His holy intervention. He longs to bring those walls down so that you can fully immerse yourself in His Word and begin to apply it as never before.

That's what He wants, you know—total immersion. He wants you to be saturated by His Word in much the same way the farmer's seeds are saturated by the rain. Remember, the Bible is loaded with tools that you, His precious child, can use to chisel away at those walls you've built to protect yourself. So, don't let anything keep you from the blessing of absorbing those precious words. Face your Jericho head-on, and bring it down with a triumphant shout!

The Last Word

In Catherine Marshall's remarkable novel *Christy* (loosely based on her mother's testimony), she shares the story of a young woman who travels deep into the mountains of Appalachia to work as a schoolteacher in 1912.

From the moment she arrives in Cutter Gap, Christy's new life presents challenges at every turn. There are so many differences between the mountain people and herself that she feels like a complete outsider. They begin to treat her as such, which doesn't help. Her peace flies right out of the window as things begin to go very, very wrong between them. She wants to turn and run, not circle the city with a trumpet in hand.

Are you sensing a theme here? There are walls between Christy and the very people she's hoping to minister to. In Cutter Gap, she faces her very own personal Jericho and doesn't have a clue how to bring the walls down.

With the help of a Quaker woman named Alice Henderson, Christy learns not to judge the people but rather to love them. She begins to see the beauty in their way of living and is eventually able to bring the walls of division down, truly becoming the teacher she had hoped to be.

Bringing walls down isn't easy, but living at peace with others is worth the effort. Getting into the Word will help. So, bring down all of those walls to saturate yourself in the very scriptures that will help you live at peace with others.

Week 2: DAY FIVE
PEACE FROM DEEPER
ENCOUNTERS WITH HIM

After trekking through the desert with the Israelites, God called Moses to meet Him on Mount Sinai, where something remarkable happened. As the Lord arrived on the scene, several newsworthy events happened in tandem: The mountain was enveloped in a cloud and began quaking. Lightning flashes shot forth as thunder rumbled in the distance. Wow! When God comes on the scene, the whole landscape changes!

In Moses' case, the following happened:

> Then Moses climbed the mountain to appear before God. The LORD called to him from the mountain and said, "Give these instructions to the family of Jacob; announce it to the descendants of Israel: 'You have seen what I did to the Egyptians. You know how I carried you on eagles' wings and brought you to myself. Now if you will obey me and keep my covenant, you will be my own special treasure from among all the peoples on earth; for all the earth belongs to me. And you will be my kingdom of priests, my holy nation.' This is the message you must give to the people of Israel."

EXODUS 19:3–6 NLT

He goes on to lay out the Ten Commandments; but let's back up for a moment, shall we?

Moses climbed the mountain to spend time with the Lord, and God showed up in a major way. Before laying out the commandments, He started with a reminder of what He had already done for the Israelites. He had saved them from the Egyptians and parted the Red Sea. He had carried them on eagles' wings. (What a lovely image!) And He brought the people to Himself.

The Sinai experience was just that. . .an experience. If you study the whole of it, you'll see that God put on quite a show for Moses and the people. He wanted to encounter them in such a way that they would never forget. Why? Because we *do* forget. We walk away from miraculous events in our lives and lose sight of all God has done for us.

Oh, may we never forget! He will strengthen you and give you peace for the journey, but why not thank Him for the many times He's already done that?

Nothing has changed from Moses' day until now, friend! As you approach the Word of God asking for strength and peace for your journey, let Him remind you of all the many times He has cared for you in the past. Has He delivered you? Has He carried you on eagles' wings? Has He brought you to Himself? If He did it once, He will do it again.

Moses walked away from the Sinai experience a changed man. (He was literally changed! His hair turned white.) God wants you to walk away from your deep encounters changed too. He wants you to be stronger than ever before, to face life's challenges head-on. And He wants to remind you of His nearness. Why? So that, even in the face of adversity, you will have overwhelming, supernatural peace.

The Blank Page

Imagine a farmer looking out over his expansive field, trying to decide what crops he will plant this season. There are so many options, aren't there? He could choose from grains like rice or wheat to vegetables like cucumbers, potatoes, onions, or carrots. Depending on his location, he might opt to plant fruit trees like lemon or orange. Isn't it wonderful that he gets to choose based on his surroundings?

Just as a farmer makes a choice about what he will produce, so do you as a child of God. As you dig in His Word, planting it deep in your heart, you get to choose what crop you'll end up with. Do you need joy? Then plant scriptures to motivate your joy journey. Do you need faith? Then follow hard after scriptures to increase your faith. If you're in desperate need of peace, never fear! The Bible is chock-full of verses to bring peace when you most need it.

Go deeper in your prayer time with the Lord. Remember, 2 Timothy 3:16 (NLT) tells us that "all Scripture is inspired by God and is useful to teach us what is true and to make us realize what is wrong in our lives. It corrects us when we are wrong and teaches us to do what is right." With that in mind, you really can choose your verses accordingly.

No matter what you're going through in your life right now, the Word of God will plant answers that can make a lasting difference deep in your heart.

❧ *The Last Word* ❧

Do you walk the walk or just talk the talk when it comes to your Christian faith? Do you barely scratch the surface of your religious life, or do you go deep with the Lord, asking Him for all He has for you?

One woman who chose to go deep was Darlene Deibler Rose, a young American missionary who traveled with her husband to the mountainous region of New Guinea just prior to WWII in order to reach the Kapauku people for Christ. Unfortunately, when war broke out with Japan, she and her husband were taken prisoner and placed in Japanese prison camps. Her husband, Russell, passed away, sadly. Darlene survived but faced unspeakable horrors in the camp: daily threats from the Japanese, rats, filth, disease, and lack of food.

Instead of growing bitter over all that happened to her at the hands of her perpetrators, Darlene chose to go deeper and deeper with Jesus throughout the experience. His presence brought comfort, strength, and peace.

Darlene faced the executioner's sword, but her life was miraculously spared. Her depth of love for the Lord saw her through even the most harrowing ordeal.

When you read this story, are you struck by how precious the Lord was to Darlene at her point of need? He can be just as precious to you, no matter what you're walking through. As you draw close to Him, He will draw close to you. He'll strengthen you and envelop you with supernatural peace.

Week 2: DAY SIX
PEACE WHEN YOU ARE OUTSIDE YOUR COMFORT ZONE

God loves to call us outside of our comfort zones, doesn't He? But let's face it, sometimes His plans just don't make sense, at least in the moment.

Think back over your life to the many times He's asked you to do something you felt incapable of doing, yet somehow the job got done. He loves to prove Himself through you, and that should bring you great hope.

Joseph learned this lesson firsthand. A young man from Nazareth, he was simply looking for the perfect match—a wife he could grow old with, one who would give him children and a home life. He never pictured himself with a young woman who would end up pregnant before their wedding day with a child that wasn't his.

Joseph made up his mind to "put her away privately" (put an end to the relationship with Mary in a way that wouldn't draw too much attention to either of them), but something miraculous occurred before he had a chance to do that. An angel appeared to Joseph and said: "Joseph son of David, do not be afraid to take Mary home as your wife, because what is conceived in her is from the Holy Spirit. She will give birth to a son, and you are to give him the name Jesus, because he will save his people from their sins" (Matthew 1:20–21 NIV).

No doubt you're saying, "Stop. Right. There. God actually expected Joseph to marry her, in spite of her pregnancy, to face ridicule, rejection, and possible excommunication from his synagogue?"

Yes, He did. God called Joseph to step w-a-y out of his comfort zone and to trust Him with what was coming. He gave Joseph great motivation in this line from the angel: "What is conceived in her is from the Holy Spirit."

And there it is: the answer from God that changes everything. When you're sure that what He's asking you to do is actually *from* Him, conceived by His Spirit, it doesn't have to make sense in the moment. You can still have peace because you trust Him so implicitly. Why do you trust Him? Because He's proven Himself trustworthy over and over again. And it's that simple, childlike trust that will ultimately bring you great peace to get the job done.

Is God calling you out of your comfort zone? Do His instructions make no sense? Instead of panicking or hiding, take a deep breath. Remember all the times He made sense of the nonsensical before, then ask for His help, His strength, His peace as you move forward with your hand in His.

Trust in the LORD with all your heart, and do not lean on your own understanding. In all your ways acknowledge him, and he will make straight your paths.
PROVERBS 3:5–6 ESV

The Blank Page

If you've walked with God for any length of time, you've probably figured out that He's in the stretching business. He uses circumstances to pull you outside of your comfort zone partly so you can grow and partly so you can testify to all He's done through you once the stretching is over. He can use anything—a situation, another person, even a tragedy—to grow your faith and to teach you that He will never leave you or forsake you.

Of course, that doesn't mean it's easy. There are days when it's tough to stare at scriptures like Philippians 4:13 (NKJV): "I can do all things through Christ who strengthens me." Sometimes you're simply not feeling it. Ever been there? After all, being stretched like a piece of elastic pulls you far outside your comfort zone, and that can be painful. On particularly rough days, you just want to cry out, "Lord, please let me rest for a while and grow later!"

This is one of the most beautiful things about the Word of God—when it's planted deep in your heart, scriptures like this week's memory verse will sustain you even when you're not feeling it. When you're weary with trying, you can say, "The LORD will give strength unto his people; the LORD will bless his people with peace," and you will begin to sense that precious peace as it floods your heart.

In the words of Australian evangelist and author Christine Caine: "Blessed are the flexible, for they shall not snap!"

❧ The Last Word ❧

Gladys Aylward underwent a great stretching period in her walk with God. In 1932, thirty-year-old Gladys made the perilous trip across Siberia aboard the Trans-Siberian Railway to Shanxi, China, so that she could begin her work as a missionary. Upon her arrival, she worked with another missionary (an older woman named Jeannie Lawson) to found the Inn of the Eight Happinesses. They provided hospitality for travelers and shared the Gospel along the way.

God showed Gladys great favor and gave her a position as an assistant to the government of the Republic of China as a foot inspector, enforcing the new law against binding the feet of young Chinese girls. She eventually adopted several children in need and advocated for prison reform. Whew! (No doubt you're tired just reading about all she accomplished.)

The region where she worked was invaded by Japanese forces in 1938, and, in an act of total faith and reliance on God, Gladys led more than a hundred orphans over the mountains to safety. Along the way, she cared for them and led many of them to the Lord.

Talk about having to be flexible! Gladys had to reinvent herself many times over—as a missionary, a hostess, a foot inspector, a mother, and even a reformer! She was led by God's peace and strength and never gave up, no matter how hard things got.

No doubt Gladys's story gives you reason to believe you can grow and be reshaped by all you're going through too. If you don't fight the stretching, imagine how flexible you will become.

Week 2: DAY SEVEN
PEACE TO LEAD THE WAY

If you've ever been called to step out in faith, you know how scary it can be. Your heart thumps and your hands tremble, especially if you don't have a lot of backing from others. It takes an incredible boldness—one of an explorer and adventurer—to boldly go where no one in your inner circle has gone before.

One great man who was called to step out in faith and lead the way was John the Baptist. Many don't realize that John was, in his own right, a Jewish prophet of priestly origin. Most just think of him as the cousin of Jesus who served as forerunner of the Gospel and, of course, the one who baptized the Savior.

We read the beginning of John's story in Matthew 3:1–3 (NLT):

> *In those days John the Baptist came to the Judean*
> *wilderness and began preaching. His message was,*
> *"Repent of your sins and turn to God, for the Kingdom*
> *of Heaven is near." The prophet Isaiah was speaking*
> *about John when he said, "He is a voice shouting*
> *in the wilderness, 'Prepare the way for the*
> *Lord's coming! Clear the road for him!' "*

Isn't it interesting that the one who predicted Christ's coming was also predicted? The prophet Isaiah couldn't have known who he was talking about when he spoke those words about a voice crying out in the wilderness, but he spoke them by faith.

Sometimes, stepping out in faith, leading the way—as both Isaiah and John did—won't make sense. God might call you, as

He did the early explorers, to travel to places yet unseen. Or maybe He'll ask you to do something that takes you far outside your comfort zone, like share the Gospel with a neighbor who has been resistant to that message. Maybe He'll even call you to share your faith on social media, something that's getting harder for believers to do.

You might not understand when God asks something difficult of you. But if you really take the time to examine the scriptures, to study the stories of men like John and Isaiah, you'll see that godly leaders—and you are one—leave behind powerful legacies. That's what you want, isn't it. . .to leave a legacy that points to Him?

Take some time to pray today. Lay your fears aside and accept His supernatural peace as you offer up words like "Lord, use me as You will." He's waiting for a willing heart, one driven by passion for Him, not afraid of what man will think.

Let's face it—whenever you step out for Christ, people often think you're a little, well, crazy. They thought that about John the Baptist too, but he ended up making the history books in a major way. So, square those shoulders. Get brave. Anticipate God's peace to encompass you as you step out for Him.

The Blank Page

Before you're ready to head out into the vast unknown to share the Gospel, you must be secure in your faith and rooted in the Word and in prayer. Only then will you have the peace and assurance you need to get the job done.

Here are a few tips to help you as you come into your prayer, praise, and Bible memorization time:

* *Give yourself plenty of focused time with no distractions. It's quality over quantity. You might only have a few minutes per day, but they can be quality minutes.*

* *Give yourself twenty-one days to establish a new habit.*

* *Find a "prayer chair," a particular chair you use for reading the Bible/praying.*

* *Find an accountability partner.*

* *Make memorization a family affair by giving your kids a memorization goal each week.*

* *See yourself as a true student of the Word.*

* *Examine verses in different translations. When you find one that really appeals to you, memorize the verse in that translation.*

* *Do a study of the words in the scripture. Use your dictionary to see what the words mean.*

* *Listen to the Bible verses aloud on an app or record them yourself.*

Once you've spent time developing your walk with God, you can begin to think of yourself as a farmer ready to toss your seed into the ground. Your seed is the Good News, and you're ready to share it with all who might be receptive. Like John the Baptist, you'll be a legacy leaver, one who makes a difference for the kingdom of God.

The Last Word

As a child, Nabeel Qureshi probably didn't imagine he'd grow up to be a Christian evangelist, one who would travel the world, sharing a remarkable testimony of his conversion. He was raised as a devout Muslim and grew up studying Islamic apologetics. Nabeel enjoyed engaging Christians in debates. In the process of doing so, he met and befriended a believer who eventually persuaded Nabeel to examine the truth of the Bible.

Nabeel's book, *Seeking Allah, Finding Jesus,* chronicles his amazing conversion. Consider these words, which he penned as part of his testimony: "I could not put the Bible down. I literally could not. It felt as if my heart would stop beating, perhaps implode, if I put it down."

Wow! Can you imagine being that impacted by the Word of God that you literally felt you could not set the Bible down? Talk about a powerful encounter!

Nabeel went on to share the Gospel across the globe, and many came to the Lord as a result of his remarkable testimony. Sadly, he was diagnosed with stomach cancer at the age of thirty-three and died a year later. Oh, but what a remarkable legacy! To think that God called him so far out of his comfort zone, and Nabeel never hesitated. He stepped out, pushing fear aside.

You can step out too. When the Word of God becomes as precious to you as it was to Nabeel, you'll absorb it like a dry sponge. It will fortify, embolden, and forever change you; and, as a result, you will do mighty things for the kingdom of God.

Week Three:

FOCUSING ON HIM

Thou wilt keep him in perfect peace,
whose mind is stayed on thee:
because he trusteth in thee.

ISAIAH 26:3

Week 3: DAY ONE
PEACE WHEN GOD INTERRUPTS YOUR PLAN

You have everything figured out. You know exactly where you're going to go, how you're going to get there, where you're going to stay when you arrive. And then, from out of the blue, a hurricane blows in, and your plans are ruined.

Likely you've experienced something similar. Life can be pretty unpredictable, and it's easy to get frustrated when your plans are thwarted. But you serve a God who thrives on giving you peace even when your best-laid plans are interrupted, so keep your focus on Him. And remember, what the enemy means for evil, God will always use for good.

Of course, not all interruptions are bad. Sometimes, the Lord shocks us with an interruption that changes everything for the better. Check out this story from Isaiah:

> *It was in the year King Uzziah died that I saw the Lord. He was sitting on a lofty throne, and the train of his robe filled the Temple. Attending him were mighty seraphim, each having six wings. With two wings they covered their faces, with two they covered their feet, and with two they flew. They were calling out to each other, "Holy, holy, holy is the LORD of Heaven's Armies! The whole earth is filled with his glory!" Their voices shook the Temple to its foundations, and the entire building was filled with smoke.*
>
> ISAIAH 6:1–4 NLT

Talk about an interruption! No doubt Isaiah's day started out like any other. He surely didn't realize the Lord Himself would show up and show off like He did! But God encountered Isaiah in a way that would revolutionize his spiritual walk. How did Isaiah respond to this interruption?

Then I said, "It's all over! I am doomed, for I am a sinful man.
I have filthy lips, and I live among a people with filthy lips.
Yet I have seen the King, the LORD of Heaven's Armies."
Then one of the seraphim flew to me with a burning coal he
had taken from the altar with a pair of tongs. He touched my
lips with it and said, "See, this coal has touched your lips.
Now your guilt is removed, and your sins are forgiven."
Then I heard the Lord asking, "Whom should I send as
a messenger to this people? Who will go for us?"
I said, "Here I am. Send me."
ISAIAH 6:5–8 NLT

When the presence of God filled the room, Isaiah was "undone." But God confirmed to his heart (with the touch of heavenly coal brushed against his lips) that his sins were forgiven and he was usable to God. Can you imagine the peace that realization brought? In an instant, all worries were washed away along with his sins.

You can have the same peace that flooded Isaiah's soul the moment that coal touched his lips, and you can have courage to face whatever God gives you on the other side of the interruption. Stay in His Word. Dig deep and ask, "Lord, I'm here. Where are You sending me today?" Then watch as He brings that Word to life and imparts new ideas and new plans that will take you places you never dreamed!

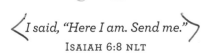

I said, "Here I am. Send me."
ISAIAH 6:8 NLT

63

❧ The Blank Page ❧

You've done a wonderful job digging into the Word over the past two weeks. You're on a journey to deepen your knowledge of who the Lord is and where He plans to take you, and you're allowing the Bible to nourish and replenish your heart to accomplish that. In many ways, you really are like a gardener. You've prepped the soil of your heart; you've readied yourself for whatever it is the Lord wants to do. Now it's time to start planting.

The gardener starts by digging a hole just big enough for the seed to fit into. That hole can't be too deep or too shallow. It must be just right. He drops in that little seed and covers it with dirt.

In similar fashion, you've allowed the Lord to root out some hard places inside of you. Now He's planting the seed of His Word in your heart as you memorize and study. He's covering it with "dirt" (His promise that it will grow).

Interruptions will still come, of course. Life will still get messy. But now that the seed of the Word is planted in your heart, you're ready to face those interruptions head-on. You can look at a bump in the road and, instead of agonizing or losing focus, say, "God has this. I know I can trust Him because Isaiah 26:3 says that God will keep me in perfect peace if my mind is stayed on Him."

Those words will come naturally and give you faith to keep going, no matter what you're facing.

❧ The Last Word ❧

History is filled with stories of people who faced interruptions to their earthly plans. One man who experienced such an encounter (or heavenly interruption) went on to change the course of Britain's history.

William Wilberforce was elected member of Parliament in 1780 as an independent. He was criticized at times for his inconsistency because he supported both the Tory and the Whig Parties. Four years later, he underwent a spiritual conversion that would revolutionize this thinking. Then, in 1785, Wilberforce faced an interruption that changed everything—his politics, his calling, even his belief system.

William's friend Gerard Edwards invited him to dinner. While there, he met the Reverend James Ramsay, a ship's surgeon, who shared a harrowing story of the appalling conditions endured by the slaves both on the plantations and at sea. Wilberforce was horrified by what he learned that night. God interrupted his neutrality with these shocking stories.

Wilberforce went on to fight to end the slave trade. It took years of battling, but the effects of his labors were felt around the globe. Talk about using a heavenly interruption for good!

It makes no sense to take the name of Christian and not cling to Christ. Jesus is not some magic charm to wear like a piece of jewelry we think will give us good luck. He is the Lord. His name is to be written on our hearts in such a powerful way that it creates within us a profound experience of His peace and a heart that is filled with His praise.

—WILLIAM WILBERFORCE, *REAL CHRISTIANITY*

Week 3: DAY TWO
PEACE WHEN SEARCHING FOR THE PERFECT FRIENDS

You were meant to live in community. The Word of God makes it clear that there's power in numbers. Matthew 18:20 (NIV) says: "For where two or three gather in my name, there am I with them." And this point is driven home in Ecclesiastes 4:9–10 (ESV): "Two are better than one, because they have a good reward for their toil. For if they fall, one will lift up his fellow. But woe to him who is alone when he falls and has not another to lift him up!"

You were never meant to do life alone. But that doesn't mean you'll never be lonely. Despite your best intentions, you've probably walked through seasons where friends seemed few and far between. And finding a good friend, one who's really got your back? Well, that's not always as easy as you might think.

The enemy of your soul wants nothing more than to discourage you in this area and to interrupt your peace by making you think no one wants to be your friend. He's a pro at causing divisions and quarrels, and he celebrates each broken friendship. But God longs for you to be surrounded with people who will lift you up when you're down and pray for you when you're going through crises. His Word is filled with glowing examples of what this could (and should) look like. Consider this friendship story from the Gospel of Luke:

One day while Jesus was teaching, some Pharisees and
teachers of religious law were sitting nearby. (It seemed
that these men showed up from every village in all
Galilee and Judea, as well as from Jerusalem.)
And the Lord's healing power was strongly with Jesus.
Some men came carrying a paralyzed man on a sleeping mat.
They tried to take him inside to Jesus, but they couldn't reach
him because of the crowd. So they went up to the roof and
took off some tiles. Then they lowered the sick man on his mat
down into the crowd, right in front of Jesus. Seeing their faith,
Jesus said to the man, "Young man, your sins are forgiven."

LUKE 5:17–20 NLT

Wow! Now those were some awesome friends with laser-sharp focus on the Savior. They would've parted the seas for their buddy. How precious, to watch him finally receive healing and wholeness.

Of course, in order to have friends like that, one has to *be* a friend like that. Today, if you're losing sleep over the "Why don't I have any true friends?" question, make up your mind to be that type of friend to others.

You can trust God in this area of your life. He has the right people out there for you. And when they do come along, watch out! Together, you'll be invincible!

"This is my commandment, that you love one another
as I have loved you. Greater love has no one than
this, that someone lay down his life for his friends.
You are my friends if you do what I command you."

JOHN 15:12–14 ESV

The Blank Page

Imagine you're walking in a garden and see one lone plant sticking up out of the ground. It sits in the center of mounds and mounds of dirt, but no other plants have grown alongside it. Seems rather odd, doesn't it? Why would the farmer put that plant alone to fend for itself?

What do you think would happen to that little plant if left to grow on its own? No doubt the wind or rain would come along and knock it to the ground. Or perhaps, without the shade of companion plants, it would wither underneath the hot sun. The stresses of life would quickly consume it, and down it would go, never to reach its full potential.

The farmer plants his seeds alongside one another so that they grow in tandem as a community. He chooses "like" seeds and plants them together, knowing they'll be stronger, healthier, and better able to grow. Their roots intertwine, stabilizing them underground so that, together, they can stand no matter what adversities come.

The same is true in your life. God has planted you next to "like" people—other believers who can lift you up when you're down. When you're struggling, they will sweep in around you, their roots running deep alongside yours. You'll feel the peace and love of your heavenly Father through the outstretched arms of the godly friends He plants next to you.

I would rather walk with a friend in the dark,
than alone in the light.
—HELEN KELLER

The Last Word

Throughout history, God has used beautiful friendships and godly relationships to spread the Gospel. Deuteronomy 32:30 tells us that one can put a thousand to flight, but two can put ten thousand to flight. Talk about strength in numbers!

God uses those numbers to impact the globe with the Gospel message. One gentleman who understood the truth of this was a Protestant missionary named Hudson Taylor. Reared in England in the mid-1800s, Hudson strongly felt the call of God to go to China. However, he knew that, as a lone missionary, he couldn't accomplish much. So, he founded the China Inland Missions, which brought in more than eight hundred missionaries to the country. (Taylor reasoned that it would take a thousand missionaries to reach the entire country and wouldn't rest until he reached that number.) Can you imagine how stressful this must have been?

And yet...125 schools were established as these missionaries worked together, and they witnessed nearly twenty thousand conversions to Christianity. Wow! There really is strength in numbers.

Today, if you're struggling to get things done on your own, stop. Go to the Word. See what the Bible says about the kind of peace you can experience when you work as a team.

Let us give up our work, our thoughts, our plans, ourselves,
our lives, our loved ones, our influence, our all, right into
His hand, and then, when we have given all over to Him,
there will be nothing left for us to be troubled
about, or to make trouble about.

—HUDSON TAYLOR, MISSIONARY AND EVANGELIST

Week 3: DAY THREE
PEACE WHEN YOUR FOCUS IS FIXED ON HIM

The thief hanging on the cross next to Jesus didn't know the scriptures. All he had to go by was the scene playing out in front of him. Yet, as he looked over at the man hanging on the middle cross, something inside of him broke. He focused on the man—Jesus—the One with the crown of thorns on His head, and was suddenly overwhelmed with emotion. "Jesus," he called out. "Remember me when you come into your kingdom" (Luke 23:42 NIV).

The One they called Jesus turned to him and, with eyes piercing his very soul, said, "Truly I tell you, today you will be with me in paradise" (Luke 23:43 NIV).

Can you even imagine the relief that must have flooded over this man as he received the forgiveness of the Savior? Talk about an eleventh-hour miracle!

You might ask yourself, "How can I stay focused on Jesus? I can't see Him with my eyes like the thief on the cross did. I can't hear Him with my ears like the disciples did." The answer is simple: read and memorize His Word. The Bible contains every bit of life instruction you could ever need. When you remain focused on the scriptures, they will help you focus on Him. It's impossible to separate one from the other!

Augustine of Hippo said, "The Holy Scriptures are our letters from home." Doesn't that present the most beautiful image ever? Jesus knew you would need peace to make it through the challenges of life. And because He's not here in the flesh to speak them into your ears, because you can't see the compassion on

His earthly face, you can turn to the Word to find verses like this week's memory verse: "You will keep in perfect peace those whose minds are steadfast, because they trust in you" (Isaiah 26:3 NIV).

The wisdom you will find in scripture will transform your thinking and radically change your life. Ultimately, the time you devote to memory work will draw you closer than ever to the Savior of the world, the One who couldn't look at the thief on the cross without seeing a child of the King.

Consider the words of Christian author and teacher Francis Frangipane:

> *To win the war against fear, we must know the true God as He is revealed in the Bible. He works to give us lasting peace. He receives joy, not from condemning us but in rescuing us from the devil. Yes, the Lord will bring conviction to our hearts concerning sin, but it is so He can deliver us from sin's power and consequences. In its place, the Lord works to establish healing, forgiveness and peace.*

That's what happens when you go to the Word, friend. When you focus on the life verses inside your Bible, you will win the war against fear. You will finally come to understand true and lasting peace, and with that understanding will come joy like you've never known before.

> *You are my hiding place and my shield;*
> *I hope in your word.*
> PSALM 119:114 ESV

❧ The Blank Page ❧

"You have to start somewhere."

Maybe you've heard or used those words. Every journey begins with the decision to start, and that's how you should approach your time in the Word. *Decide* to grow your Bible time. *Decide* to allow the passages from God's Holy Word to penetrate your heart. *Decide* to memorize, even if it seems hard. Even now, the Lord is ready to plant His seeds of truth deep in your heart so you can experience lasting peace and true transformation in every area of your life. But He can't start until you decide.

When a gardener sows seeds, he takes the seed and plants it directly into the ground as opposed to transplanting small plants that were started elsewhere. In much the same way, you've made the decision to plant the seed of the Word directly into your heart as opposed to just listening to a sermon or reading a theological book. God will honor this with much growth!

The Word was meant to be read and applied this way. It's sad to think that for hundreds of years, the church didn't have access to the scriptures for their personal study. How magnificent that it's available to us now. We can't ever take it for granted.

I believe the Bible is the best gift God has ever given to man. All the good from The Savior of the world is communicated to us through this Book.

—ABRAHAM LINCOLN

The Last Word

If we have any one man to thank for putting the Bible into the hands of the people, it's fifteenth-century theologian Martin Luther. Luther started his journey in the Catholic Church as an Augustinian monk. He struggled with the tenets of the faith and tried to open the floor for discussion but was eventually ostracized from the church.

Luther's teachings differed from the church of his day in this way: he believed that salvation and eternal life weren't earned by good deeds but were a free gift born of grace and could be found only in a personal relationship with Jesus. Most of us would agree with that.

Luther decided the people needed to learn for themselves what the Word of God had to say and not just lean on their church leaders to interpret it for them. (Bold move, wouldn't you say?) His translation of the Bible into German as opposed to Latin opened the door for millions to read and understand the Word of God for themselves.

Think about that for a moment: if not for the bravery of one man, you might not have personal access to the Bible. What a gift he gave the church. His courage literally changed the course of the world. That's how strongly he felt about the scriptures, and that's how strongly we should feel about them too. Today, as you set out to memorize and apply the words of the Bible to your current situation, thank God for the opportunity to read and study the Word for yourself.

Week 3: DAY FOUR
PEACE WHEN GOD IS SPEAKING

If you've been walking with the Lord for a while, you've probably discovered that He speaks to His children through His Word, through His still, small voice, through circumstances, and sometimes through miraculous encounters.

Consider the story of Deborah, an Old Testament prophet. Despite being a woman, she was a judge in Israel who rendered her judgments underneath a date palm tree in the land of Ephraim. God spoke to Deborah and gave her a specific word, which she shared with a military commander named Barak. She encouraged him to muster ten thousand troops and concentrate them on Mount Tabor. The Lord told Deborah that He would draw Sisera, an oppressive commander of the Canaanite army, to Mount Tabor, where the battle would be fought.

Barak agreed to go but only if Deborah went with him. Stop to think about that for a moment. The commander of the army wouldn't move unless the woman who gave him the word went with him. That's how strongly we should feel about facing our battles too. When we receive a word from the scriptures or any other way, we shouldn't move without carrying that word with us. This is one reason it's so important to memorize the scriptures that can alter your life. You can take them into battle with you, just as Barak did.

Deborah agreed, and together they headed to Mount Tabor. Barak had nothing to fear, for the Lord spoke through Deborah, saying,

"Go! This is the day the L$_{ORD}$ has given Sisera into your hands. Has not the L$_{ORD}$ gone ahead of you?" So Barak went down Mount Tabor, with ten thousand men following him. At Barak's advance, the L$_{ORD}$ routed Sisera and all his chariots and army by the sword, and Sisera got down from his chariot and fled on foot. Barak pursued the chariots and army as far as Harosheth Haggoyim, and all Sisera's troops fell by the sword; not a man was left.

JUDGES 4:14–16 NIV

Read those verses again. Barak not only relied on the word he had received; he acted on it. And because he acted on it, the enemy was defeated.

What is God's word for you today? What battles are you facing? Who or what is standing on your Mount Tabor? Is it an enemy that looms over you, terrifying you and making your knees knock? If so, get a word! Go to the Lord and ask Him to direct you to a specific passage that you can stand on, one that will motivate, propel, and empower you to take down your Sisera.

If you read the fifth chapter of Judges, you'll see a victory hymn that Deborah and Barak sang together after the battle was won. You'll be singing a victory hymn too once you garner the courage to stand on the Word and face your battles head-on. No doubt that hymn will sound something like this: "Lord, You've kept me in perfect peace as I've focused my heart and mind on You, even in the midst of the battle. I will follow hard after Your Word, Lord, and keep my trust in You. Together, we are victorious, Father!"

The soul can do without everything except the word of God, without which none at all of its wants are provided for.
—MARTIN LUTHER, *ON CHRISTIAN LIBERTY*

The Blank Page

Who tells the gardener what to plant, when to plant it, and how it should be done? He relies on multiple things—the climate in his area, the type of soil, and the stories he hears from other farmers/gardeners in his area. He wants a word from others who've gone before him, so that he doesn't make the same mistakes they made.

If you're looking to move forward in life and not get stuck in the same ruts as before, listen to the testimonies of those who've already made progress in the areas you want to explore. You need a word! And you don't have to look any further than *the Word* to find it!

If you're struggling with jealousy, read the story of Rachel and Leah or the tale of two brothers—Jacob and Esau. If you're battling pride, check out some of those Old Testament kings. If you're trying to overcome addiction, read the story of Gomer (from the book of Hosea). She battled an addiction that almost ruined her marriage, but God brought restoration and peace.

He'll do the same for you if you lean in and listen to the word He's trying to share through the lives of these great men and women of faith. In all of these stories, you'll find the encouragement you need to get past your Mount Tabor and find lasting peace.

The fact that God is infinite makes the study
of His Word a lifetime occupation.
—Billy Graham

The Last Word

Perhaps no musical artist has impacted contemporary Christian music culture more than Keith Green. This extraordinarily gifted musician had a radical conversion in the mid-seventies. He could have used his talents to sing anything he wanted. Indeed, he garnered a secular record deal with Decca Records when he was only eleven years old. But when the Lord impacted Keith's life, He did so in a way that changed everything, including Keith's passions.

Keith was one of those people who encountered God in such a powerful way that it transported his music and his lyrics. The Lord imparted song after song, almost like a computer downloading files, into Keith's spirit. Those songs went on to change not just one but multiple generations for the Lord. Even though Keith died at the age of twenty-eight, his music lives on because of the power and the spirit behind it.

That's what happens when God speaks. His Word changes literally everything. It changes who you are, what you do, and who you will become. Its transformative power will alter not just your life but the lives of those you come in contact with. That's why it's so important to get the Word of God into your heart and mind. And it's also why the enemy works so hard to keep you away from the Bible.

You might not be a Keith Green, but God wants to impact your circle of influence. Today, take the time to get into His Word as never before, and let its words alter your life.

Week 3: DAY FIVE
PEACE THAT FUELS PASSION

We find a remarkable story repeated in several of the Gospels. Here's a peek from the book of Luke:

> *And a woman was there who had been subject to bleeding for twelve years, but no one could heal her. She came up behind him and touched the edge of his cloak, and immediately her bleeding stopped.*
>
> *"Who touched me?" Jesus asked.*
>
> *When they all denied it, Peter said, "Master, the people are crowding and pressing against you."*
>
> *But Jesus said, "Someone touched me; I know that power has gone out from me."*
>
> *Then the woman, seeing that she could not go unnoticed, came trembling and fell at his feet. In the presence of all the people, she told why she had touched him and how she had been instantly healed. Then he said to her, "Daughter, your faith has healed you. Go in peace."*
>
> LUKE 8:43–48 NIV

Can you imagine the inner turmoil this woman must have faced? For twelve years, she had been ostracized by her community and was forced to live on the fringes of society. For twelve years, she could touch no one, experience no human contact whatsoever. And for twelve years, she had struggled with the pain and other symptoms of her physical and emotional malady.

Twelve years is a long time to suffer. Maybe you can relate. Perhaps you deal with a chronic illness or emotional issue that has taken equally as long to resolve, and you wonder if an answer will ever come.

The key to this woman's healing was her passion to reach the Savior. The moment she placed eyes on Him, all of her fears dissipated. One glance convinced her the answer was on its way. But she had to take a step of faith to reach it.

Have you ever been fueled with passion that drove you to God for an answer to a problem you faced? If so, then surely you understand the supernatural peace that accompanies such passion. Even the meekest person can do remarkable things when emboldened by the Spirit of God.

Take another look at this week's memory verse (Isaiah 26:3), this time in the New Living Translation: "You will keep in perfect peace all who trust in you, all whose thoughts are fixed on you!"

There's no promise in that verse that hard times won't come. Oh, but when they do, you can fix your thoughts on God. You can be driven by His Spirit straight into the Savior's arms. The story might not resolve in the way you expected, but it will ultimately bring a deeper, more intimate relationship with Him. And the transformative peace will astound you.

If you've been passionless, take some time today to ask God to reinvigorate you with His Spirit. Then, just as the woman with the issue of blood, press in. Don't stop until you reach the hem of His garment.

The Blank Page

Check out this beautiful verse from Luke: "They said to each other, 'Didn't our hearts burn within us as he talked with us on the road and explained the Scriptures to us?'" (Luke 24:32 NLT).

Have you ever had that sensation? Maybe you were sitting in church and the pastor shared a story that "quickened" your heart. Or maybe you were listening to a worship song when tears began to flow. The same thing can happen as we open the Bible. A verse can come alive in our spirits and radically change us in an instant. God can move us to great passion with just a word when His Spirit is behind that word.

That's what happened to the disciples as they traveled on the road to Emmaus just a few short days after their friend Jesus died. In the middle of their mourning, a stranger joined them and began to reveal several key scriptures from the Old Testament—prophecies about the resurrection of the Savior. Not realizing they were talking to Jesus, the men were "quickened" in their hearts by the words this man spoke. Something about His words resonated with them, and they experienced a physical manifestation.

When was the last time your heart burned within you as you heard the words of Jesus? When were you fueled by holy passion to do or say something that came straight from Him? When did you experience supernatural peace that you knew without a shadow of a doubt came from Him? If it's been too long, spend time with the Lord today, and ask for a fresh outpouring of His Spirit.

The Last Word

When you're fueled by passion for God, it's impossible to quit. People might try to deter you, but you will not be stopped. In many ways, this passion is like a car with the engine revving. It causes the believer to move forward with little fear about the outcome.

One man who experienced such passion was John Bunyan, author of *Pilgrim's Progress*. Bunyan had a passion for the Word of God. To quote Charles Spurgeon, "If you cut him (John Bunyan), he'd bleed Scripture!"

Bunyan took those seeds of passion and fanned them into a flame for God and for the people who needed to know God. After serving in the British army, he married and became profoundly interested in the church. However, he wasn't content with the status quo. In fact, Bunyan became a "nonconformist" during a period of time when doing so meant risking his freedom.

Unwilling to curtail his preaching, Bunyan was arrested and spent twelve years in jail. (Wow! Think about that. . .the same length of time the woman suffered with the issue of blood.)

Propelled by supernatural peace, Bunyan refused to give up. There was too much work to be done. After his release from jail, he continued spreading the Gospel, publishing not only *Pilgrim's Progress* but nearly sixty sermons as well.

Perhaps you read his story and think, "Wow, I wish I had that kind of passion." It can be yours, friend! Spend time in God's Word and in His presence. Ask for a fresh outpouring, and then expect an overflow. The Lord wants nothing more than to fuel you for the work ahead.

Week 3: DAY Six
PEACE TO WALK ON WATER

If you had asked Peter, the disciple of Jesus, about the things he hoped to accomplish in his lifetime, surely "walk on water" wouldn't have made the list. In fact, he'd probably never even considered the notion that a human being could accomplish such a thing.

Here's the story of how and why that well-known walk took place.

Immediately Jesus made the disciples get into the boat and go on ahead of him to the other side, while he dismissed the crowd. After he had dismissed them, he went up on a mountainside by himself to pray. Later that night, he was there alone, and the boat was already a considerable distance from land, buffeted by the waves because the wind was against it.

Shortly before dawn Jesus went out to them, walking on the lake. When the disciples saw him walking on the lake, they were terrified "It's a ghost," they said, and cried out in fear.

But Jesus immediately said to them: "Take courage! It is I. Don't be afraid."

"Lord, if it's you," Peter replied, "tell me to come to you on the water."

"Come," he said.

Then Peter got down out of the boat, walked on the water and came toward Jesus. But when he saw

the wind, he was afraid and, beginning
to sink, cried out, "Lord, save me!"

Immediately Jesus reached out his hand and caught
him. "You of little faith," he said, "why did you doubt?"

MATTHEW 14:22–31 NIV

This week's memory verse could have been written with Peter in mind. He learned by experience that Jesus would keep him in perfect peace as long as he kept his focus on Him. And consider this: Peter had to exhibit a keen amount of trust just to step out of the boat in the first place. No doubt, his legs were a wobbly mess as he made that first step. Yes, he lost his focus for a moment and started to go down. But what an act of bravery!

God will call you out of your proverbial boat on many occasions. You'll have to step out in faith even when your knees are knocking. But, like Peter, you will make it as long as your eyes remain fixed on His. And somehow, peace will come though storm waters make your journey precarious.

Consider this quote by Simone Weil: "If three steps are taken without any other motive than the desire to obey God, those three steps are miraculous; they are equally so whether they take place on dry land or on water."

What boat do you need to step out of today? Jesus is waiting on the other side of your faith, arms extended.

"Be strong and courageous. Do not fear or be in dread
of them, for it is the LORD your God who goes with
you. He will not leave you or forsake you."

DEUTERONOMY 31:6 ESV

The Blank Page

How does the gardener know that a seed will sprout into a plant? How can he be sure that, year after year, a crop will come forth from once-barren land? After years of trial and error, he learns to trust the process. The gardener's faith journey begins at the point where he drops that seed into the ground and covers it with soil.

The same is true in your life. When you bump up against problems, there are things you can and should do to remedy the situation. But there comes a time when you have to take your hands off, step back, and say, "God, I trust You with this, and I'm leaving it to You."

When you plant those seeds of faith, peace will come. Hebrews 11:1 (ESV) says: "Now faith is the assurance of things hoped for, the conviction of things not seen." The gardener has the assurance of things hoped for. . .and so do you.

The key, as always, is to remain fixed on Jesus. And that's why staying in the Word is so critical when you're going through problems. Instead of sinking like Peter almost did, you can have the "assurance" (confidence, promise, positive declaration) that God will work everything together for your good (Romans 8:28).

You've planted so many seeds of faith along the way. Are you truly anticipating the crop yet to come? Don't give up. God wants to surprise you with a bountiful harvest.

The Last Word

Sometimes when Jesus asks you to step out of the boat, He's leading you to something bigger than anything you might have imagined. Such was the case with a young woman named Lottie Moon.

Lottie experienced a spiritual awakening in her teens. Though single women weren't generally welcomed on the mission field in the mid-1800s, she and her younger sister, Edmonia, both eventually accepted the call to become missionaries in North China.

God asked Lottie to step out of the boat on multiple occasions, and she did so willingly. But stepping out wasn't easy. Over the many years in ministry, she faced all sorts of hardships, including famine, plagues, revolution, and even war. This precious woman of God cared so deeply for the people under her care that she was willing to do anything to help them. When famine came, she begged the missions organization for more money, but there was no additional money to be had. Without her fellow missionaries and friends knowing, Lottie gave of her own food and finances to care for those in need, ultimately taking a toll on her health and shortening her life.

God's way isn't always the easy way, but it's always the right way. No matter what He calls you to do, you can trust Him. Drop those seeds of faith into the ground as you step out in faith, then press your fears aside as He takes you places you never dreamed of.

Only believe, don't fear. Our Master, Jesus, always watches over us, and no matter what the persecution,
Jesus will surely overcome it.
—LOTTIE MOON

Week 3: DAY SEVEN
PEACE WHEN TEMPTATIONS COME

Was there ever a more idyllic setting than the Garden of Eden? There, in that lush place, Adam and Eve had everything they could have possibly wanted—fresh food, a gorgeous environment, all of nature and the animal kingdom at their disposal, and, best of all, constant communication with their Creator. They truly had it made. Why, then, did they succumb to temptation when that sneaky snake reared his ugly head? Why trade perfection for imperfection? Who would do that?

The enemy of your soul is subtle. He's tricky. He knows how to get you to shift your focus from the promises of God to his "alternate plan." Only the outcome is never as he promises. Instead of peace and tranquility, you find yourself in turmoil, far from God. Perhaps this is why Jesus, in the Lord's Prayer, added the line: "And lead us not into temptation, but deliver us from evil" (Matthew 6:13). He understood that the ultimate goal of Satan was to separate man from God and to destroy his peace in the process.

Maybe you know what that feels like. You've followed hard after God, giving your heart to Him and studying His Word. Then temptations came. A friend invited you to a party you shouldn't have attended. Someone of the opposite sex said "all the right things" to land you in a compromising position. In the end, you found yourself far from God, peace a thing of the past.

In his book *Mere Christianity*, C. S. Lewis said:

*A silly idea is current that good people do not
know what temptation means. This is an obvious lie.
Only those who try to resist temptation know how
strong it is. . . . A man who gives in to temptation
after five minutes simply does not know what it
would have been like an hour later. That is why bad
people, in one sense, know very little about badness.
They have lived a sheltered life by always giving in.*

Do his words resonate with you? Do you usually give in? If so, it's not too late. The Lord has a plan for moments of temptation. Just as Peter kept his gaze on Jesus, you can choose to turn your eyes to Him in the very moment of temptation.

Pull out those verses you've been memorizing. Use them as strategic weapons to fight the temptations right away. Peace will flood your soul when the "I have to give in" feeling finally passes. And oh, how good you'll feel to step away and say, "Whew! I really dodged a bullet!" With God's help, you can dodge them all.

*Now the serpent was more crafty than any of the wild animals
the Lᴏʀᴅ God had made. He said to the woman, "Did God really
say, 'You must not eat from any tree in the garden'?"*

<small>Gᴇɴᴇsɪs 3:1 ɴɪᴠ</small>

❧ The Blank Page ❧

It's tempting to sleep in, to pull the covers over your head and skip your morning time with God. Who would blame you? You work so hard, and your life is so overwhelming. You need the extra rest.

No doubt the farmer feels the same way as he faces that empty field. The work ahead will be exhausting, and he must get started early in the day if he's going to finish on time. So, he pushes the covers back, swings his legs over the side of the bed, and gets going, whether he feels like it or not.

You won't always feel like it either, but here's the wonderful thing about meeting with God first thing in the morning: you'll kick the day off right with your prayer and Bible time, and the rest of your day will be much smoother as a result.

Consider these words from Psalm 5:3 (NLT): "Listen to my voice in the morning, LORD. Each morning I bring my requests to you and wait expectantly."

Why do you suppose it's easier to meet with God in the early morning hours? Because the cares of the day haven't rushed in to meet you yet. There, in that quiet, peaceful place, He can flood your soul with His presence and greet you with a fresh word, perfect for the day, one that will propel you with peace.

How wonderful to start your day with Him!

The Last Word

"The vigor of our spiritual life will be in exact proportion to the place held by the Bible in our life and thoughts." Those words were spoken by a remarkable man of God named George Müller, a nineteenth-century evangelist passionate about working with orphans. George was supremely interested in prayer and concluded that anything and everything should be taken to the Lord for consideration. He fully expected his heavenly Father to answer every single prayer.

Time and time again, God came through for George. The miraculous stories are many, but one stands out: When the orphan house boiler stopped working, it was deemed beyond repair. No problem. Müller believed that if he prayed, the issue would be solved, even though the weather called for the use of the boiler. He prayed specifically that the weather would abate. . .and God answered. The boiler was fixed as the winds blew in a different direction, away from the orphanage.

Because he refused to give in to the temptation to quit praying and reading the Bible, Müller's faith increased day by day. In fact, it's said that he spent hours a day praying and reading the Word. In his golden years, he read through the Bible four times each year. Wow!

Answers are found in the Word, so it's easy to see why the enemy would try to keep you from it. Be like George. Trust God, no matter the circumstances. Spend quality time reading the Bible, applying its truths, and praying for direction from the Lord. This is His greatest desire: to spend daily time with you, His child.

Week Four:

PEACE iN YOUR RELATiONSHiPS

If it be possible, as much as lieth in you, live peaceably with all men.

ROMANS 12:18

Week 4: DAY ONE
PEACE WHEN YOU'RE UPSET AT OTHERS

Live at peace with all men. . .and women. Maybe you read those words and think, "Yeah, right. If God only knew the people I have to put up with, He wouldn't ask that of me!" Oh, but He does know, and He wants you to try anyway.

Take a closer look at this week's memory verse: "If it be possible, as much as lieth in you, live peaceably with all men" (Romans 12:18).

Three things become clear when you break down this verse: First, you have to acknowledge that some relationships are truly impossible. There are people who are so toxic that you can't be around them. There are others who can remain but don't need to be in your inner circle. Second, consider the second phrase "as much as lieth in you." Because some people demand so much of you, you get to decide who stays and who goes, who's close and who's not. You should analyze every friend who crosses your path: Is this one a keeper? Is it possible to sustain a relationship with this person and not lose my sanity? Finally, read the last part of the verse: "live peaceably with all men." To live peaceably doesn't mean you won't have conflict. And it also doesn't mean you live as a doormat. It simply means that you resolve your issues in a godly manner and keep moving forward.

So, what do you do when conflict comes? How do you make peace? Consider this verse from Matthew 5:9 (NIV). Jesus said, "Blessed are the peacemakers, for they will be called children of God." Notice He says "peacemakers" and not "peacekeepers." There's a huge difference between the two. A peacekeeper will end up getting used (and possibly abused) because she doesn't ever stand her ground. But a true peacemaker will create lasting peace by speaking the truth in love, even when it's difficult.

Jesus was a peacemaker. Remember the story of Mary and Martha from Luke 10:38–42 (NIV)?

As Jesus and his disciples were on their way, he came to a village where a woman named Martha opened her home to him. She had a sister called Mary, who sat at the Lord's feet listening to what he said. But Martha was distracted by all the preparations that had to be made. She came to him and asked, "Lord, don't you care that my sister has left me to do the work by myself? Tell her to help me!"

"Martha, Martha," the Lord answered, "you are worried and upset about many things, but few things are needed—or indeed only one. Mary has chosen what is better, and it will not be taken away from her."

Martha wanted to nitpick and complain that her sister wasn't helping enough. Jesus could've whispered in Mary's ear, "Go on over there and help your sister clean just to shut her up. It will pacify her." Instead, He called Martha to task, didn't He! How awkward she must have felt when Jesus said, "Mary has chosen what is better." But Jesus knew that Martha needed to learn a lesson, and He taught it to her by "making" the peace.

As you set out to memorize this week's verse, ask yourself: Am I a peacekeeper or a peacemaker?

Above all, keep loving one another earnestly, since love covers a multitude of sins.

1 PETER 4:8 ESV

The Blank Page

Have you ever heard the term *companion planting*? Sometimes a farmer will deliberately place very different plants alongside each other in the garden. For instance, he might sow a plant that attracts pollinators alongside another plant in need of pollination. He might plant garlic next to broccoli or cauliflower because it will help with bug control. The same is true when he plants parsley next to carrots, peas, or tomatoes. The companion plant plays a role in protecting and/or nourishing the others. Put the wrong plants together and. . .watch out! Some are real bullies, stealing all of the nourishment from the other!

Just as the farmer puts unrelated plants together to benefit one another, so God plants you in relationships with the people in your circle. Over time, you will begin to realize the benefit as you discover your friends' unique roles in your life, and they are discovering your worth too!

Take another look at this week's memory verse. Personalize it by saying it this way: "Lord, if it's possible, as much as I'm able, I'm going to do my best to be a peacemaker with all who cross my path." See how you were able to make that verse come alive?

Plants need excellent companions to thrive, and so do you. If you're in a relationship that's draining you, move on! Plant yourself deep next to those who will help guard, guide, and protect you with their love.

The Last Word

"So, you are the little woman who wrote the book that started this great war."

According to legend, Abraham Lincoln spoke these words to Harriet Beecher Stowe when they first met. Her novel, *Uncle Tom's Cabin*, had depicted the horrendous truths of slavery and had changed the course of American history. But her story really began before the writing of that book. It started with a vision she had of a dying slave.

Harriet was so moved by this vision that she wrote to the editor of a weekly antislavery journal with these words: "I feel now that the time is come when even a woman or a child who can speak a word for freedom and humanity is bound to speak. . . . I hope every woman who can write will not be silent."

Does that sound familiar? Jesus could have kept silent when He saw Martha's sin. He could have ignored it and hoped she would eventually learn on her own. But He did the brave thing. He spoke up, and it changed Martha's life and probably Mary's too.

Harriet Beecher Stowe could not be silent about the sin of slavery. She had to speak up. Doing so probably meant she lost a few friends. Oh, but the ones she gained must have been far better. And her bravery landed her in the history books.

Is it time for you to speak up? Have you allowed someone else's sin to go on too long? Lean on this week's verse as you contemplate how the Lord wants you to move forward.

Week 4: DAY TWO
PEACE TO OVERCOME RELATIONAL ISSUES

If you've read the story of twin brothers Jacob and Esau from the twenty-fifth chapter of Genesis, you probably remember that they struggled with each other in the womb. Sibling rivalry even before birth!

Jacob came out of the womb holding on to his older brother's heel. No doubt he had a "little brother" complex most of his life. And it didn't help that his father favored Esau, who was a hunter. Mom clung tight to Jacob, so it might be fair to say he was a bit of a mama's boy. Talk about the potential for relational disaster. These two brothers were as different as could be!

Things came to a head with the two brothers when Esau, famished from working in the fields, came to Jacob and begged him for a bowl of stew. Jacob agreed but threw in the words "Only if you agree to give me your birthright." Ouch. That seems like a high price to pay for a bowl of stew, doesn't it? But Esau went along with it, his stomach propelling the story forward.

Later, Rebekah and Jacob devised a plan to deceive Isaac, who pronounced a blessing on the wrong son. Jacob became the favored one, and Esau went down in the history books as the one who foolishly sold his soul for a bowl of soup. Can you imagine the deep regrets he must have faced in the years following that foolish decision?

Maybe you read this story and you're reminded of a relationship with one of your siblings. Maybe you've battled jealousy or animosity with one or more of your brothers or sisters. It happens, especially in close quarters during childhood. But things can get sticky even as adults. Political differences, jealousies, frustrations. . .these things can all put up walls between siblings that are hard to tear down.

Consider this quote from author Pamela Dugdale: "Siblings are the people we practice on, the people who teach us about fairness and cooperation and kindness and caring—quite often the hard way."

When you think about it that way, it's easy to see why there are so many squabbles between brothers and sisters growing up. They're practicing on each other!

Think about your siblings or close relations as you work on memorizing this week's verse. Ask yourself: If it's at all possible, as much as it lies within me, can I live peaceably with my siblings and other loved ones? Answering "yes" might mean you have to do the hard work of having a difficult conversation with one or more of them. But you'll be following in the footsteps of Jesus, your Peacemaker, when you do.

Love one another with brotherly affection.
Outdo one another in showing honor.
ROMANS 12:10 ESV

The Blank Page

A winter squash can take 45 to 55 days to fully mature after flowering. This would make its total journey about 80 to 120 days, if you count the time from seed planting to flowering. Contrast that with radishes, which morph from seed to harvest in four weeks. Wow, they're fast!

It's the same with siblings. Some take a long time to mature, while others seem to get there overnight. Some enter adulthood with childish behaviors, while others seem like grown-ups from the time they're children.

When you see the different maturity levels of siblings, it's easy to figure out why disagreements rise among them. You might process things completely different from your sister or brother simply because you're on a different maturation plane.

Living at peace with others often means you have to look past "where they are" to their hearts. And remember, instead of fretting over how immature your loved ones are, you might want to consider doing a personal maturity check to make sure your reactions aren't too over-the-top.

Check out this lovely quote from writer and church leader Mike Yaconelli: "I just want to be remembered as a person who loved God, who served others more than he served himself, who was trying to grow in maturity and stability."

If we all felt that way, sibling rivalry and, indeed, all relational issues would fade away, and we truly could live at peace with all people.

❧ The Last Word ❧

Growing up with a contentious person in the house is never easy. Maybe you can relate. Perhaps you had an angry father or a bitter, complaining mother. Maybe your younger sister was sassy and talked back. Maybe your older brother rebelled against your parents and turned to drugs or alcohol. Or maybe you were the contentious one, never happy with your situation. These types of behaviors can make everyone uncomfortable, can't they?

Now imagine you're growing up in the home of someone with a completely different belief system than your own. You believe in God, but your sibling doesn't. Or, harder still, your parent or child doesn't.

Such was the case with William J. Murray, son of the now infamous Madlyn Murray O'Hare, the atheist activist who petitioned to have prayer and Bible reading removed from public schools in the early 1960s. In spite of his mother's convictions that the Almighty did not exist, William grew up to discover God on his own. He went on to become an author, minister, and political lobbyist.

William rose above the surroundings in which he grew up, and the Lord used his upbringing as part of his testimony. God can, as the saying goes, turn any test into a testimony, even rocky relationships. So, hang in there. The Lord wants to bring you peace, no matter how contentious things in your home might be at the moment.

> *Peace is a daily, a weekly, a monthly process,*
> *gradually changing opinions, slowly eroding*
> *old barriers, quietly building new structures.*
> —JOHN F. KENNEDY, FINAL ADDRESS TO
> THE UNITED NATIONS GENERAL ASSEMBLY

Week 4: DAY THREE
PEACE IN THE WAITING

How long would you be willing to wait on your miracle? Would you give up after one year? Two? Ten?

Sarah, wife of Abraham, remained childless until she was ninety years old. Allow that to sink in for a moment. God had promised the couple a child and had even told Sarah she would be the mother of nations, but His promise was not fulfilled for years.

Sarah got ahead of God while waiting. She gave Abraham her maidservant, Hagar, and encouraged them to produce a child together. They did. Ishmael was born, but he wasn't the child of promise the Lord had referred to. That's what happens when you are impatient and try to fix things outside of God's will: you end up with an illegitimate result that only leads to more bitterness and envy.

Filled with fear and doubt, Sarah didn't think she would ever see the fulfillment of God's promise in her own life. She had all but given up. Take a look at how Sarah handled the waiting. Instead of trusting, instead of being overwhelmed with God's peace, she tried to find a way to fix the situation: "If I can't give Abraham a child, I know someone who can."

Maybe you're a fixer too. You don't wait very well. You get impatient. You stop trusting, stop hoping, and find yourself anxious and upset, pointing fingers at God.

The Lord repeats His promise to Sarah in Genesis 18:10–15 (NIV). Look at how she responds:

Now Sarah was listening at the entrance to the tent,
which was behind him. Abraham and Sarah were
already very old, and Sarah was past the age of
childbearing. So Sarah laughed to herself as
she thought, "After I am worn out and my lord
is old, will I now have this pleasure?"

Then the LORD said to Abraham, "Why did Sarah laugh
and say, 'Will I really have a child, now that I am old?' Is
anything too hard for the LORD? I will return to you at the
appointed time next year, and Sarah will have a son."

Sarah was afraid, so she lied and said, "I did not laugh."

But he said, "Yes, you did laugh."

Here's the thing: Sarah could have chosen to have peace in the waiting. She could have resolved in her spirit to hand the reins to God as she waited. But being the impatient sort, she went a different route.

What about you? When you're waiting on the Lord, do you give up easily? Do you lose your peace when the miracle is long in coming? If so, take a look at this week's memory verse from a completely different angle. Read it this way: if it be possible, as much as lieth in you, live peaceably with the Lord while waiting on Him to move. The truth is you'll get along better with others if you're reconciled to Him, even in the waiting.

The LORD is good to those who wait for him,
to the soul who seeks him.
LAMENTATIONS 3:25 ESV

❧ The Blank Page ❧

Oftentimes, a farmer will plant what's known as a *cover crop*. These are fast-growing plants such as grains, legumes, or grasses. Why does he do this? Because they have soil-enhancing properties. The farmer will place them in the soil and then remove them before they produce seed, simply for the enhancement.

Wow! Sounds a lot like what God does in our hearts, doesn't it? While we're waiting on Him (before the crop is ever planted), He prepares us. He gets us ready. He sends people to speak words of faith over us so we don't give up. He points us to scriptures like Isaiah 40:31 (ESV): "But they who wait for the LORD shall renew their strength; they shall mount up with wings like eagles; they shall run and not be weary; they shall walk and not faint."

As we read those words, they jump out at us as a reminder that He hasn't forgotten us and is faithful to keep His promises. We breathe a sigh of relief, knowing we can trust Him even in the waiting.

Today, ask the Lord to plant scriptures in your heart that will help during "waiting seasons." This cover crop will keep you going until you see the fulfillment of His promise in your life.

The Last Word

Waiting on God is never easy, but imagine you had to do it from behind prison walls. Such was the case with Corrie ten Boom, a Dutch Christian watchmaker who was sent to a concentration camp for helping Jews escape from the Nazis during World War II.

Corrie endured countless hardships in that horrible place but managed to keep believing, trusting, hoping, even after the death of her precious sister, Betsie. She never gave up on God's promise that He would redeem the situation.

Fifteen days after Betsie's death, Corrie was released. She later learned that her release had been a mistake, a clerical error. Less than a week later, all the women in her age group were put to death in the gas chambers.

Can you imagine God asking Corrie to memorize this week's verse? "If it be possible (*in a gas chamber?*), as much as lieth in you (*even after the death of a beloved sister?*), live peaceably with all men (*even Nazis intent on taking my life?*)."

Consider these words from Corrie in her book, *The Hiding Place*, to see how she dealt with one of her tormenters:

> *Even as the angry vengeful thoughts boiled through me, I saw the sin of them. Jesus Christ had died for this man; was I going to ask for more? Lord Jesus, I prayed, forgive me and help me to forgive him. . . . Jesus, I cannot forgive him. Give me your forgiveness.*

Friends, what a message! God never said it would be easy to live at peace with people, simply that it was possible, even in the waiting.

Week 4: DAY FOUR
PEACE IN THE PIT

If you have brothers and sisters, you've probably experienced sibling rivalry. This is especially true when parents play favorites. If anyone understood what it felt like to be Dad's favorite, Joseph did.

Now Israel loved Joseph more than any other of his sons, because he was the son of his old age. And he made him a robe of many colors. But when his brothers saw that their father loved him more than all his brothers, they hated him and could not speak peacefully to him.

GENESIS 37:3–4 ESV

Sounds great if your name is Joseph. But those other eleven brothers had different names. None of them got a robe. None of them got special attention like Joseph did. And none of them felt like putting up with Joseph's perceived bragging when he shared a dream about how they would all one day bow down to him.

Deciding enough was enough, this motley crew tossed baby brother into a pit. "They saw him from afar, and before he came near to them they conspired against him to kill him. They said to one another, 'Here comes this dreamer. Come now, let us kill him and throw him into one of the pits'" (Genesis 37:18–20 ESV).

If it wasn't for the fact that their intentions are clear ("conspired against him to kill him"), you might almost write off this pit toss as a prank. But these brothers were genuinely filled with revenge.

Of course, God turned the story around. One brother believed they should spare his life. Instead of killing him, they sold Joseph to a caravan of Ishmaelites passing by. Joseph was taken to Egypt, and the Lord used his time there to work remarkable miracles. You probably know how the story ends. The brothers—in need of food—traveled to Egypt. In the end, not recognizing their own now-grown brother, they did, indeed, bow down to him.

God has a sense of humor, doesn't He? He can take what your enemy or even your family members meant for evil and use it for your good. That doesn't make things any easier in the moment of conflict; but if you remain focused on Him, if you're patient in the waiting, you will see a lovely payoff.

Think about this week's memory verse (Romans 12:18) in light of Joseph's story. "If it be possible (*even in the pit*), as much as lieth in you (*even if your own brothers hate you and want you dead*), live peaceably with all men (*forgive, and watch God perform a miracle*)."

If Joseph could forgive his brothers for wanting him dead, no doubt you can forgive your siblings for the things they've done to hurt you over the years. That's God's heart for your family, of course—to forgive and move forward. It is possible to live peaceably with those who've hurt you. Does this mean you have to be BFFs? Maybe not. But it does mean you have to forgive and then ask for holy intervention from your heavenly Father, who longs to heal what's broken.

Let brotherly love continue.
HEBREWS 13:1 ESV

The Blank Page

Read any *Farmer's Almanac*, and you'll stumble across the term *hardening off*. To harden off a plant means you slowly get it used to outdoor conditions. Plants sown indoors are gradually acclimated to the outdoors over a period of days, maybe even a week. If indoor-sown plants aren't acclimated, they'll never survive once placed outside in the soil.

The same is true with people, even those inside your own family. Let's say you're praying for a brother who doesn't know Jesus. You can't just slam-dunk him with truth. He's liable to run in the opposite direction. You have to garner his trust and his love over a period of time, and then, when the moment is right, his heart will be ready.

This acclimation process is fascinating because we're not privy to God's timetable. He knows when things will work out, but we do not, which is why we have to remain diligent and patient, even in the waiting. In the meantime, if that brother is belligerent toward your faith, you can remain steadfast, loving, and calm. You can "live peaceably" with him by not deliberately stirring him up when his heart is clearly not ready.

Oh, but when that plant is ready to go into the soil, nothing can stop it from growing! The farmer's wisdom has given that little plant an optimal chance for survival. You can do the very same thing.

Not always eye to eye, but always heart to heart.
—Anonymous

The Last Word

"Do not hinder me if you will not help. Perhaps, if you had kept close to me, I might have done better. However, with or without help, I creep on." In 1785, elder brother John Wesley penned these difficult words in a letter to his younger brother, Charles.

Why? Charles had been publicly critical of John's leadership in the Methodist Church. Ouch! It's one thing to criticize a sibling in private, another to take it to the airwaves.

Maybe you've been there. A sibling has radically different political beliefs than you. He's very vocal on social media. You're not. But you get rankled every time he makes a post, because it flies in the face of what you believe to be true. So, you comment on a post, and chaos ensues.

How do you live at peace with a sibling you disagree with? Simple. Back away from the fire. Never take your battles public. Remember, Matthew 18:15 (ESV) says: "If your brother sins against you, go and tell him his fault, between you and him alone. If he listens to you, you have gained your brother."

There's a reason God never intended people to publicly ridicule one another. It goes against everything Jesus preached. So, don't use your passion to fan into flame an argument with a brother, especially not in public. No one wins that way. Instead, read that verse you've been memorizing all week. Learn to live at peace with all men and women by not making a scene.

Week 4: DAY FIVE
PEACE WHEN YOU'RE OUT OF YOUR ELEMENT

Even those who are not well-versed in the Bible usually know the following familiar verse: "Whither thou goest, I will go; and where thou lodgest, I will lodge: thy people shall be my people, and thy God my God" (Ruth 1:16).

These words were spoken to Naomi, a wonderful mother-in-law, by a brokenhearted young woman named Ruth who had just lost her husband. Naomi's husband had just passed away too, so the women were bonded in pain. According to the story, Naomi released both of her daughters-in-law (Orpah and Ruth) to return to their own people after the deaths of their respective husbands. Orpah chose to go back home, but in a stunning move, Ruth opted to go to Bethlehem with her mother-in-law.

Think about that. She was choosing to leave everything and everyone she knew to travel to a place she'd never been—a place with a different culture, different people, different religion. Such was her love for Naomi. Ruth simply couldn't break the relationship, even if it meant starting over in a new place.

Once in Bethlehem, Ruth went to work in the field of a man named Boaz, a relative of Naomi's. There, she risked being molested by the men working the field alongside her. Fortunately, Boaz showed her favor and kindness. He gave his workers specific instructions to leave her alone. Ruth was able to relax under his care. Eventually, Boaz claimed Ruth as his own and covered her with the hem of his garment (a symbolic move to represent his emotional, provisional, and spiritual covering),

It would have been easy for Ruth to fight the process once she arrived in Bethlehem. She could have said, "I'd rather not work in the field with a group of strangers, thanks just the same." But she didn't. Knowing she had to protect and guard her mother-in-law, whom she loved, she was willing to sacrificially lay down everything.

Ponder her attitude in light of this week's memory verse (Romans 12:18). "If it be possible (*in spite of losing your husband*), as much as lieth in you (*even while grieving and facing life-changing decisions*), live peaceably with all men (*even in a foreign land among those who are culturally different*)." What an example to us all! It's possible, even in the middle of the upheaval, to be at peace.

Ruth went on to marry Boaz, and she's one of five women counted in the lineage of Jesus. She could have chosen to return home to the comfort of her family, but God used her decision to form a family line that eventually led to the Savior of the world.

*L̲O̲R̲D̲, my heart is not proud; my eyes are not haughty.
I don't concern myself with matters too great or too awesome
for me to grasp. Instead, I have calmed and quieted myself
like a weaned child who no longer cries for its mother's
milk. Yes, like a weaned child is my soul within me.*
PSALM 131:1–2 NLT

Most apple, pear, cherry, and plum trees thrive in cold weather. But, put an orange tree in an Alaskan field, and it won't stand a chance. Oranges thrive in the south because they require a lot of sunlight. They do best in temperatures between 55 and 100 degrees Fahrenheit.

Orange trees go dormant in the wintertime when temperatures begin to fall below 55 degrees. But any colder than 35 degrees, and you have a problem on your hands. Freezing temperatures will destroy the fruit.

Think about that for a moment as it applies to your spiritual life. God wants you to thrive outside of your comfort zone.

Don't be an orange tree. Make up your mind to flourish regardless of where He plants you. Even if you're surrounded by people who are unfamiliar or unkind, it's still possible to thrive. Begin to memorize verses like Philippians 4:11: "Not that I speak in respect of want: for I have learned, in whatsoever state I am, therewith to be content."

The point is, unlike that fruit tree, you can adapt and can live at peace with the new crowd as you learned to do with the old one.

And remember, farmers have learned little tricks to help their plants acclimate in unfamiliar climates. They often use a device called a cold frame—a four-sided frame with a clear top—that raises the temperature of the garden and tricks those plants into believing they're in a southern state.

God will place a cold frame around you too, even when people are giving you the cold shoulder. He'll place the perfect people in your path who will welcome you with open arms.

The Last Word

William Booth (known as "the General") founded the Salvation Army in 1878. But he didn't work alone. He had the full support and participation of his wife, Catherine, who became known as "the Mother of the Salvation Army." She was, in her own right, a tremendous preacher. Catherine's work with alcoholics was admirable. She helped many through the conversion process and into wholeness and healing.

Though she was completely out of her element, Catherine persevered. She went to places where few people dared go and ministered to people most would ignore. She met practical needs by providing food, and she saw others as equals in the kingdom. As a traveling evangelist, her impact on the kingdom of God was great. Many would agree that she was as popular as her husband, William. She drew large crowds when she spoke, and the Lord used her mightily.

Interesting, isn't it? God took this housewife and mother of eight so far out of her comfort zone to the heart of people with addictions, financial issues, and other glaring problems. He'll do that with you too if you allow Him. He'll give you a heart for the needy, the downtrodden, those in pain. God will remove your fear as He encourages you to step far out of your comfort zone to meet them where they are.

With the help of Romans 12:18, you can truly live at peace with all people, even those from radically different situations than your own. That's the heart of Jesus, after all.

Week 4: DAY SIX

PEACE WHEN YOU FEEL THE STING OF BETRAYAL

Hang around people long enough, and sooner or later you'll feel the sting of betrayal. It's especially hard when the betrayer is someone you're very close to. Nothing hurts worse than a knife in the back from a friend.

Jesus knew what this felt like, of course. His disciple Judas turned on Him and betrayed Him for thirty pieces of silver. Ouch.

You'll face many Judases in your life as well. How you respond to these unexpected and painful betrayals says a lot about your character and your relationship with Christ. If you can avoid the knee-jerk response, your heart will be guarded from further injury.

Let's look at this week's memory verse (Romans 12:18) in light of betrayal: "If it be possible (*even when your heart is broken*), as much as lieth in you (*even though you're stunned and confused because you trusted this loved one*), live peaceably with all men (*even the very one who betrayed you*)."

So, how does that work? Does God intend for you to go on with the relationship as if nothing had happened? Absolutely not. The answer to that question is found in Matthew 18:15–17 (NLT):

> *"If another believer sins against you, go privately and point out the offense. If the other person listens and confesses it, you have won that person back. But if you are unsuccessful, take one or two others with you and go back again, so that everything you say may be confirmed by two or three witnesses. If the person still*

refuses to listen, take your case to the church. Then if
he or she won't accept the church's decision, treat that
person as a pagan or a corrupt tax collector."

These days, of course, people rarely handle friendship disputes this way. They put up walls. They attack on social media. They rally the troops against the one who offended them. But you can be different. If you really want to learn to live at peace with others, you have to be willing to follow God's plan for restoration and reconciliation.

Consider this quote from author and speaker Brené Brown in her book *The Gifts of Imperfection*: "Shame, blame, disrespect, betrayal, and the withholding of affection damage the roots from which love grows. Love can only survive these injuries if they are acknowledged, healed and rare."

Of course, not every friendship can be mended after a break, but that's okay too. God can use what the enemy meant for evil for good in your life. You can grow from the experience and use it as you move ahead into other friendships.

"And whenever you stand praying, forgive, if you have
anything against anyone, so that your Father also who
is in heaven may forgive you your trespasses."
MARK 11:25 ESV

The Blank Page

When God plants the seed of His Word in your heart, it takes root and changes you. You're then able to face hard situations from a different perspective—that of the Creator of the world. It becomes a filter through which you view everything, even betrayal.

Perhaps it's getting easier to see why Bible memorization is key to your growth as a believer in Jesus Christ. When the filter of the Word is firmly in place, every situation you walk through becomes easier.

Today, take the time to analyze your memory growth. Have you figured out new ways to get and keep the scriptures in your heart and mind? Are those techniques helping you? Are you, like the gardener, planting seeds and truly believing for a good outcome?

Consider the story of a pastor from Texas named John. He was skilled at Bible memorization, absorbing whole chapters. Later in life, John developed Alzheimer's disease. Still, at his wife's prompting, he could quote whole passages from the Bible, completely clearheaded.

That's the power of the Word of God, friend. Plant it deep in your heart, and it will never fail you, even if your body does. It will survive the tests of time, trauma, and betrayal and will feed your soul every step of the way.

> *The words of the Bible have life! God works through these words. The Bible is to God what a surgical glove is to the surgeon.*
> —MAX LUCADO, *ONE GOD, ONE PLAN, ONE LIFE*

The Last Word

It's one thing to feel the betrayal of one person, but what if you faced the opposition of a whole tribe? In 1962, Don Richardson left his home in Canada with his wife and seven-month-old baby to work with the Sawi tribe in Dutch New Guinea. This was no quick, easy decision. The Sawi were known to be cannibalistic headhunters. Don realized that he was putting his life in danger but followed the leading of the Lord to move anyway.

The Richardsons lived in isolation from the modern world and were exposed to a variety of illnesses. There was also the constant threat of violence. Still, they persevered and learned the native language, a daunting task.

It didn't take long for Don to realize that three tribal villages were in a never-ending battle with each other. This prompted him to make the decision to leave with his family, except something remarkable happened to change everything. Hearing that he was leaving, the Sawi people came together and made a peace pact with their enemies. They underwent ceremonies in which young children were exchanged between the villages as a sign of peace.

When Don and his wife saw how broken and contrite the people were, they decided to stay. As a result of this act of forgiveness among the tribes, many villagers came to know Christ.

Wow! What a story. God can truly bring peace, even in the middle of pain, hurt, and betrayal. If He can mend fences between whole tribes, imagine what He can do in your relationships!

Week 4: DAY SEVEN
PEACE WHEN YOU'RE INEXPERIENCED

Has God ever used you to serve as a mentor in someone's life? Maybe He led you to someone younger than yourself who needed direction. Or perhaps He brought a new believer into your path, someone older than yourself but young in the faith. It feels good to pour out of what you've learned, doesn't it? And it feels good to be mentored as well. Tremendous relationships are formed by mentors and mentees.

The Bible shares a story of just such a relationship between the apostle Paul and young Timothy, his protégé. Timothy, who hailed from Asia Minor, watched as his Jewish mother converted to Christianity. The young man followed suit, giving his heart to the Lord as well.

Paul was on his second missionary journey when he met Timothy and took him under his wing. Timothy became Paul's friend, companion, and coworker. He traveled with Paul and Silas and was the recipient of the first and second epistles of Timothy.

Young Timothy must have struggled with feelings of insecurity at some point along the way, because we read an interesting passage in Paul's first letter to him: "Don't let anyone look down on you because you are young, but set an example for the believers in speech, in conduct, in love, in faith and in purity" (1 Timothy 4:12 NIV).

Paul encouraged the young man to look past his inexperience, to put his faith and trust in God, who had all the experience he could ever need. Knowing he could lean on the Lord and not his own experience surely brought Timothy great comfort and peace.

It should bring you peace too! Instead of looking at the areas of your life where you don't quite measure up, look at how far God has brought you. Look at how open your heart is to watching Him move through you. Look at the joy you've experienced in the journey so far!

Consider this quote from educator Randy Pausch, found in his book, *The Last Lecture*: "Experience is what you get when you didn't get what you wanted. And experience is often the most valuable thing you have to offer."

It takes time to garner the experiences that will mold and shape you into the person you want to become. In the meantime, be at peace! God is already working in and through you, and He certainly doesn't look down on you because of your youth or inexperience.

Now consider Timothy's situation through the lens of this week's memory verse (Romans 12:18): "If it be possible (*and it is, thanks to the help and encouragement of my mentor*), as much as lieth in you (*my confidence is boosted, thanks to his encouragement*), live peaceably with all men (*as my mentor is demonstrating through his daily actions*)."

This is how God wants us to live, friend! Lasting peace is truly possible when we develop strong and lasting relationships with godly people who want to see us reach our potential in Christ.

Therefore be imitators of God, as beloved children.
EPHESIANS 5:1 ESV

The Blank Page

Think about this: Seeds have never been plants before. They don't know how to grow. They come into the process completely inexperienced. Yet, a gardener never looks at a seed and says, "I don't think I'll use you. You don't look like you know what you're doing."

That happens to people sometimes, doesn't it? The boss advances the obvious person—the one winning all the accolades. But there are other wonderful people ready to learn and grow, standing right there, getting overlooked. It's not fun. In fact, it stinks. How can you prove your worth if no one ever gives you a chance?

God wants us to be equal opportunity friends and companions to those around us. He doesn't want us to overlook anyone. The youngest, most inexperienced person could turn out to be your Timothy! He or she could change the world if given the opportunity.

Today, if you're struggling with feeling overlooked, lean on this verse: "But seek first the kingdom of God and his righteousness, and all these things will be added to you" (Matthew 6:33 ESV). When you put the Lord in His rightful place, He'll take your seed of faith and grow it to the point of usability. Then, you'll do unstoppable things for Him! In the meantime, follow the advice of Winnie the Pooh, who said, "You can't stay in your corner of the Forest waiting for others to come to you. You have to go to them sometimes."

The Last Word

Neurosurgeon Ben Carson became the director of pediatric neurosurgery at the Johns Hopkins Children's Center at the age of thirty-three. Wow! For one so young, he had a plethora of life experiences. He's best known for performing the only successful separation of conjoined twins at the back of the head. He also performed the first successful neurosurgical procedure on a baby still inside the womb. Talk about talent!

Carson went on to run for president of the United States and to serve as HUD (Housing and Urban Development) director. But his story really begins many, many years before that, when he was just a child.

Ben grew up in a home with a strong mother, one who wouldn't allow a victim mentality. He has said of her: "I had a mother who would never allow herself to be a victim no matter what happened. . . . Never made excuses, and she never accepted an excuse from us. And if we ever came up with an excuse, she always said, 'Do you have a brain?' And if the answer was yes, then she said, 'Then you could have thought your way out of it.'"

Growing up in the inner city of Detroit, it would have been easy for Ben to feel overlooked. But thanks to a strong and confident mentor (mom), he thrived and went on to do remarkable things with his life. God will use you to do great things too, no matter how humble your beginnings. Don't allow the victim mentality to creep in. Keep a hopeful heart, your focus fully on the Lord.

Week Five:

PEACE LEADS TO THANKFULNESS

And let the peace of God rule in your hearts, to the which also ye are called in one body; and be ye thankful.

COLOSSIANS 3:15

Week 5: DAY ONE
PEACE WHEN HEALING COMES

Imagine you've prayed for a miracle for years. A financial break-through. A physical healing. A wayward child in need of salvation. Then, miraculously, God answers your prayer. . .just like that. After all that waiting, the moment has finally arrived, and you're in shock that it happened so quickly and unexpectedly.

How do you respond when you finally get what you want? Do you celebrate? Share the news with others? Do you keep plowing forward, forgetting all of the years of prayer that went into that miracle?

Here's a terrific story from Luke 17:11–19 (NLT). God is hoping this very real illustration will propel you to return to Him with thanks after He's performed a miracle on your behalf.

As Jesus continued on toward Jerusalem, he reached the border between Galilee and Samaria. As he entered a village there, ten men with leprosy stood at a distance, crying out, "Jesus, Master, have mercy on us!"

He looked at them and said, "Go show yourselves to the priests." And as they went, they were cleansed of their leprosy.

One of them, when he saw that he was healed, came back to Jesus, shouting, "Praise God!" He fell to the ground at Jesus' feet, thanking him for what he had done. This man was a Samaritan.

Jesus asked, "Didn't I heal ten men? Where are the
other nine? Has no one returned to give glory to God
except this foreigner?" And Jesus said to the man,
"Stand up and go. Your faith has healed you."

Can you see things from Jesus' perspective? He's worked a miracle not just for one person but ten. Talk about generosity! Imagine you had ten children, and you gave each of them an expensive gift for Christmas, but only one returned to thank you. It would feel pretty lousy, wouldn't it? Oh, but one came back. And his words must have touched Jesus' heart.

The moral of this story? Be the one who comes back. When God moves on your behalf, return and thank Him. Praise Him for the work He's done. Don't take it for granted. Don't gloss over it. When you live a life of gratitude, you'll always walk in peace with God, for gratitude leads to peace.

If you're still waiting on your miracle, it's not too soon to praise the Lord. Follow the advice in this quote: "For one minute, walk outside, stand there, in silence. Look up at the sky and contemplate how amazing life is" (Anonymous).

There's always something to be grateful for. And when you begin to see life in that way, you will be flooded with peace in the moment, which is exactly what you need while you're waiting.

Oh give thanks to the LORD, for he is good,
for his steadfast love endures forever!
PSALM 107:1 ESV

The Blank Page

Can you imagine the joy in a gardener's heart when he sees that first little shoot poking out of the ground? All of that work, all of that backbreaking effort, is finally going to pay off. The teensy-tiny pop of green is enough to make his heart sing with joy.

Picture the gardener's revelation in light of this week's memory verse from Colossians 3:15: "And let the peace of God rule in your hearts, to the which also ye are called in one body; and be ye thankful." God loves it when we show gratitude in the little things. He's doing a proverbial happy dance alongside the one who's celebrating. That little pop of green makes His heart happy too! And never underestimate the role that thanksgiving plays in your peace journey. They walk hand in hand, very comfortable companions.

Think of all the times God has moved on your behalf. Begin to thank Him even now! Use this week's memory verse as a springboard for praise and thanksgiving for all He has done. Here are some areas you might list: finance, health, family, friendships, job, and habits. Take a look at each of those categories and acknowledge all the Lord has done in and through you over the years. Then, as you offer up words of praise for the miracles He's performed, peace will surely flood your soul and invigorate you to hope for the miracles you're still waiting on.

The Last Word

Helen Keller wasn't born deaf, mute, and blind but contracted an illness at the age of eighteen months that left her in such a state. Family members thought the little girl's situation was hopeless, that she would never be able to communicate with them. Then Anne Sullivan arrived on the scene. She was a gift to the Keller family, one sent straight from heaven.

Helen would later refer to the day of Anne's arrival as "my soul's birthday" for it was the day hope entered the home. Sullivan began the arduous process of teaching Helen sign language. It took a full month before Helen had a breakthrough. As Anne ran cool water over Helen's hand, she spelled out w-a-t-e-r in her palm with hand motions.

Recounting the story, Helen said, "I stood still, my whole attention fixed upon the motions of her fingers. Suddenly I felt a misty consciousness as of something forgotten—a thrill of returning thought; and somehow the mystery of language was revealed to me. I knew then that w-a-t-e-r meant the wonderful cool something that was flowing over my hand. The living word awakened my soul, gave it light, hope, set it free!"

What happened in the next few minutes was, indeed, miraculous. Helen nearly wore Anne out, demanding the names of other familiar objects around the home.

Can you imagine what a joyous day that must have been and how thankful the entire family was for Anne's diligence? Before long, they settled into a peaceful routine where Helen continued to learn. She was the first deaf-blind person to earn a bachelor of arts degree and went on to become an author, political activist, and lecturer. Her life was a miracle, born of thanksgiving!

Week 5: DAY TWO
PEACE WHEN PROVISIONS ARE LOW

There's a remarkable story in the seventeenth chapter of 1 Kings. The prophet Elijah was without provision during a season of drought. God instructed him to go to the town of Zarephath, explaining that a widow woman would care for him there.

Elijah did as instructed and asked the woman (a total stranger) for water and bread.

"As surely as the Lord your God lives," she replied, "I don't have any bread—only a handful of flour in a jar and a little olive oil in a jug. I am gathering a few sticks to take home and make a meal for myself and my son, that we may eat it—and die."

Elijah said to her, "Don't be afraid. Go home and do as you have said. But first make a small loaf of bread for me from what you have and bring it to me, and then make something for yourself and your son. For this is what the Lord, the God of Israel, says: 'The jar of flour will not be used up and the jug of oil will not run dry until the day the Lord sends rain on the land.'"

She went away and did as Elijah had told her. So there was food every day for Elijah and for the woman and her family. For the jar of flour was not used up and the jug of oil did not run dry, in keeping with the word of the Lord spoken by Elijah.

1 Kings 17:12–16 niv

Can you imagine the faith it must have taken for the woman to prepare that small loaf of bread for Elijah? And can you picture her surprise as the bag of flour continued to replenish itself and the jug of oil never ran dry?

God hasn't changed. According to Hebrews 13:8, He's the same yesterday, today, and forever. If Jehovah Jireh (your Provider) cared for Elijah, He will care for you. Doesn't it bring peace to your soul to realize He has you covered? Now you can read this week's memory verse and really feel it all the way down to your toes. His peace can rule your heart, even when you're struggling financially, and you can be thankful, even before the provision comes.

That's the key, by the way. You can begin to thank Him for the miracle before you see it with your eyes. In a way, that's what Elijah was doing when he made the trek to Zarephath. By going there, he was saying to God, "I see what You're up to, and I trust You, so I'm stepping out in faith." That kind of faith always leads to miracles and to a sense of security, peace, and trust in your always faithful Jehovah Jireh.

And my God will supply every need of yours according to his riches in glory in Christ Jesus.
PHILIPPIANS 4:19 ESV

✿ The Blank Page ✿

If you wish to plant a flower garden in an area of your yard that receives full sunlight, you choose annuals or perennials that thrive with lots of light. Choices might include dahlias, peonies, chrysanthemums, geraniums, or lavender. These flowers drink in the sunlight. Many of them require six to eight hours of sunlight per day, in fact.

You're just like those plants. You thrive in the sun (er, Son). You need adequate time to drink in His presence, just like those plants absorb all they need from the light. That's why you can't rush through your time in the Bible or in prayer. You must imagine you're like a dry sponge, ready to soak it all in, just as those plants beg for the warmth of the sun on their colorful faces. When you take the time to do that, the Word of God comes alive in your spirit. The words on the pages become more than mere words. They are life. They are light. They are nourishment.

If you put full-sunlight plants in a shaded area, they eventually die. Without their lifeline, they simply can't make it for long.

Neither can you. If you're feeling drained or sluggish in your faith, make sure you're getting adequate Son-light.

The Last Word

World-renowned surfer Bethany Hamilton thrived in the sunlight from the time she was a child. Even as a very little girl, she couldn't wait to get on her board and paddle out.

That hasn't changed now that she's grown, but her situation looks a little different. In 1990, while on her surfboard, she was attacked by a shark and lost her left arm.

For others, this might have been too much to handle. Many with weaker faith would have turned their faces to the wall and cried out, "Why me, Lord!" and never tried again. That has never been Bethany's style. She's a young woman of great faith who has always trusted in God. She turned her face to the Son and drank in His promise that He would provide all she needed—not just to surf again but to compete.

Bethany went on to do great things both on the water and off. Her testimony served as the foundation for a terrific movie, and she has been an inspiration to millions of young people struggling through hard times.

Jehovah Jireh met her at her point of need, didn't He? And check out this amazing statement of faith, straight from Bethany's lips: "I wouldn't change what happened to me because then I wouldn't have this chance, in front of all of you, to embrace more people than I ever could have with two arms."

You can experience the same supernatural peace, no matter what you're going through. Get alone with God and cry out to Him. Acknowledge your lack and give Him the opportunity to provide what you need. He longs to meet you no matter where you are.

Proverbs 29:2 (NLT) tells us that "when the godly are in authority, the people rejoice. But when the wicked are in power, they groan." Put a godly team in authority, and the country prospers. Remove that covering, and the people struggle.

One of the more prominent, effective kings in Old Testament history was a man named Hezekiah, who reigned between c. 715 and 686 BC. According to 2 Kings 18:5 (ESV), "He trusted in the LORD, the God of Israel, so that there was none like him among all the kings of Judah after him, nor among those who were before him." So great was his legacy that Hezekiah was included in the lineage of Jesus.

What made this king so great, and what can we learn from him to apply to our own lives in our journey toward lasting peace? Hezekiah enacted sweeping reforms that forbade the worship of false deities within the temple of Jerusalem. He mandated for the sole worship of the one true God, Yahweh! Hezekiah also purified and repaired the temple. He abolished idolatry and insisted the country remain focused on God.

Wow! That's a lot, isn't it? There's more to Hezekiah's story, including a miraculous intervention of God that saved his life in later years; but for the sake of our study, let's focus on his godly rule and reign over Israel.

We're not always blessed to have godly rulers in charge, are we? And when the evil reign, it's easy to get discouraged. They can make things very difficult for the body of Christ. During these seasons, we often lose our peace and begin to walk in fear.

God wants you to trust Him, no matter who is in office. He wants you to see that these "reigns" are only temporary. In light of eternity, they are but a drop in the bucket. Still, He always wants us to clearly see that revival can come when the godly rule, which is one reason it's important to vote according to the Bible.

What does true revival look like? Just as in the days of Hezekiah, it means pushing out anything that doesn't honor God. It means lifting His name both in our private prayer and worship time and in the public square. It means we open ourselves to the supernatural intervention of God in our lives, our neighborhoods, our communities, our states, and our country. Ultimately, it means that we put the Lord in His rightful place.

Today, as never before, begin to pray for revival in the land. Glean from 2 Chronicles 7:14 (NIV), which reads: "If my people, who are called by my name, will humble themselves and pray and seek my face and turn from their wicked ways, then I will hear from heaven, and I will forgive their sin and will heal their land."

He will, you know, and He will bring supernatural peace in the process.

Will you not revive us again,
that your people may rejoice in you?
PSALM 85:6 ESV

The Blank Page

Just as a country prospers when the godly rule, so does the garden of your heart prosper when you place it under the tender, loving care of the Master Gardener. If you want true revival to come, you don't have to wait until all is right with the world. It can begin today, in this very moment, in fact.

To prepare your heart for revival, spend time with the Lord in prayer. Repent of any sins you might still be holding on to. Let them go. Then turn to the Word as never before. Absorb it like a thirsty camel in the desert. Ask God to bring the passages to life. Lean on this week's memory verse, and apply it to your life in a personal way with this prayer:

God, now that I've let go of the things that held me back, I give You full reign in my heart! I ask You to overwhelm me with Your peace. I choose to praise You and trust in You, even if life isn't perfect. I'm so thankful for what You are doing, Lord. Please revive my heart, my mind, my spirit. Breathe on me, Spirit of God, and do a fresh work in my heart, I pray. Amen.

God longs to do all of those things and more. He wants to captivate you with His presence and to bring you hope, no matter what you're walking through. Today, all of that can be yours if you just dig into His Word and ask Him to bring it to life in your heart.

❧ The Last Word ❦

Fanny Crosby, the great hymn writer, faced many challenges in her life. A mistake at the hands of a misguided doctor caused her to go blind as an infant. What should have been a simple infection turned into a lifelong disability because of his negligence.

Some might have lashed out, angry at the doctor or filled with bitterness at their unfair plight. But not Fanny! Instead, she considered her blindness to be a blessing. Instead of complaining or worrying about everything she couldn't do, she decided to give God all the praise.

Fanny longed for true revival, and it came as God poured out lyrics for hymn after hymn. Led by the Spirit of God, Fanny wrote between 5,500 and 9,000 hymns, many of which are still sung today. Her legacy began with a mistake, a problem that would have derailed someone of lesser courage. But it ended with a gift that has spread from generation to generation, inspiring and encouraging the masses.

Fanny allowed the peace of God to rule in her heart as she recognized the calling He had placed on her life. She expressed thanksgiving and praise in every lyric, her life a genuine reflection of Colossians 3:15.

God wants no less for you. No matter what hardships you're facing, true revival can still come. Allow the very thing the enemy meant for bad in your life to propel you into the arms of the Savior. He will revive your heart, your mind, and your spirit.

PEACE WHEN YOUR PERSPECTIVE IS ADJUSTED

To have a change of perspective means you shift the way you look at things. Maybe you can't help but look at a season of financial loss as devastating, but God can adjust your perspective and cause you to see it as a season of hope and trust in Him. Or maybe you look at a chronic illness as a curse, when the Lord wants to show you how you can begin to see it as a blessing, a way of connecting with others who are also struggling.

If anyone knew what it was like to have his perspective adjusted, it was a New Testament man named Zacchaeus. As the chief tax collector in the town of Jericho, he was probably not well liked. Add to that the complication of his short stature, and you can see that Zacchaeus had a lot going against him. When he heard that Jesus was coming through town, Zacchaeus worked his way through the crowd and fixed his gaze on a sycamore tree. He made a quick decision to shimmy up that tree so that he could have a closer look at the Savior.

When Jesus got to that area, He looked straight up into the tree, where Zacchaeus probably thought he was out of sight. Jesus called him by name, instructed him to come down out of the tree, and said, "I'm going to your house today."

Wow! Can you imagine? The crowd was probably flabbergasted by this proclamation. How could Jesus, a religious teacher and prophet, go to the house of a tax collector? Would the Savior of the world really dine with sinners?

Oh, but God wanted to change not just Zacchaeus's perspective of himself but the community's as well. By acknowledging him (calling him by an actual name instead of "tax collector") and by offering to visit his home, Jesus was showing the community that He loved everyone equally. This must have shaken the Pharisees in the bunch, don't you think?

Zacchaeus saw his situation from a whole new perspective after his climb up the tree. No longer hiding under the stares of the locals, he was now physically and psychologically elevated to position of equal.

God longs to change your perspective too. How else can you have peace when you're going through tough times if not for obtaining His point of view, His way of looking at things? And remember, the choice is yours: "The only thing you sometimes have control over is your perspective. You don't have control over your situation. But you have a choice about how you view it" (Chris Pine). Today, choose a brand-new way of looking at things. Doing so will change everything.

As we look not to the things that are seen but to the things that are unseen. For the things that are seen are transient, but the things that are unseen are eternal.

2 Corinthians 4:18 esv

✿ The Blank Page ✿

How do you view your Bible memory time? Is it a drudgery, something you dread? Or is it fun and imaginative, filled with possibilities for life-changing encounters with the Word of God? The Lord wants you to approach your time in His Word with zeal and passion, not like a kid waiting for a math test. If your perspective doesn't change, it's going to zap all the joy out of what could be a delightful process.

When the farmer drops those seeds into the ground, he's not thinking, "Ugh! This is such a pain!" He's already thinking of the crop those seeds will produce and how it's going to provide for his family. He's completely peaceful, looking forward to a great harvest.

You need to think about the "produce" of your spiritual field in the same way. Don't look at your memorization work as, well, work. Look at it as a beautiful, rich field that will produce a harvest that will change your life and potentially the lives of your family members. And remember, this "perspective adjustment thing" is a lifelong process. With every little shift, you're becoming more and more who He meant you to be all along. So, take it slow and easy, memorizing in workable chunks. God will honor your diligence as your attitude and perspective gently adjust to His plan and His Word.

The remedy for discouragement is the Word of God.
When you feed your heart and mind with its truth,
you regain your perspective and find renewed strength.
—Warren Wiersbe, clergyman and Bible teacher

The Last Word

"Perspective is everything when you are experiencing the challenges of life." These words might seem commonplace until you realize they were spoken by Joni Eareckson Tada. This amazing woman of God was born in 1949 in Baltimore, Maryland. She lived a very active life.

On July 30, 1967, Joni dove into the Chesapeake Bay. She misjudged the depth of the water. When she hit the bottom of the bay, she suffered a fracture between the fourth and fifth cervical levels and instantly became a quadriplegic. This meant she went from being athletic and physically strong to losing all feeling from the shoulders down.

You can imagine how a person's perspective might change for the worse, should an accident like that occur. And she did go through two years of doubts while rehabilitating and struggled with depression.

God began to change Joni's perspective when she learned to paint using a brush between her teeth. This led to other achievements, including writing. To date, she's written more than forty books!

With this perspective shift came a passion to reach others in similar situations. She founded Joni and Friends in 1979, a ministry to people with disabilities and their families. God has used an accident that many would consider a tragedy to accomplish much good.

What area of your life needs a perspective shift today? Ask the Lord to give you a whole new way to look at your situation so that you can begin to do great and mighty things for Him.

PEACE THAT LEADS TO CELEBRATION

There's a fascinating story in the third chapter of the book of Acts, one that should bring you such hope! Peter and John were just approaching the temple gate called Beautiful, when they came across a man who was lame from birth. He asked them for money, but check out Peter's swift reply:

> *Then Peter said, "Silver or gold I do not have, but what I do have I give you. In the name of Jesus Christ of Nazareth, walk." Taking him by the right hand, he helped him up, and instantly the man's feet and ankles became strong. He jumped to his feet and began to walk. Then he went with them into the temple courts, walking and jumping, and praising God. When all the people saw him walking and praising God, they recognized him as the same man who used to sit begging at the temple gate called Beautiful, and they were filled with wonder and amazement at what had happened to him.*
>
> ACTS 3:6–10 NIV

Can you imagine? One minute, unable to walk, the next, walking and jumping and praising God! This guy went from zero to fifty in just a few seconds' time! And how good of the Lord to give him more than what he asked for!

Are you as quick to praise the Lord when He blesses you? Do you immediately see that He's the One who provided what you needed? When you've been struggling for some time and finally get your answer, no doubt you feel like jumping and dancing too! This is especially true when the Lord goes above and beyond, blessing you in ways you never expected and possibly feel you don't deserve. He lavishes His children with His love and is deserving of a joyous response from a grateful heart. So, dance away! Leap! Run! Praise!

God loves to hear a song of praise from your lips. There's such joy, such peace, from a heart filled with praise for Him—not just when He blesses but also when things are rough. So, don't wait until the blessing comes. Make a joyful noise no matter where you are.

Today, determine to remember that every good gift comes from Him. He's placed you at Gate Beautiful in the heart and thoughts of the Savior of the world and wants to offer you something far more valuable than money. He wants to give you joy unspeakable and full of glory (1 Peter 1:8, paraphrased).

Every good and perfect gift is from above,
coming down from the Father of the heavenly
lights, who does not change like shifting shadows.
JAMES 1:17 NIV

⚘ The Blank Page ⚘

When a gardener tends to his plants, he's careful to remove any dead flowers to make room for the new ones. This process is called *deadheading*. It helps the plant flower for a longer period of time. In short, it becomes more productive.

In a way, praising God is like deadheading a plant. The more you do it, the more productive you are. And remember, praise leads to praise. Once you send the praise train down the track, it's hard to get it back!

So, where do you stand on the "praising" scale? Are you a praiser? Does the notion of running and leaping and praising God sound ridiculous to you, or can you see yourself doing that? Maybe you would say, "I wasn't raised that way." That's fine, but don't let your upbringing keep you from a celebration of the spirit!

Begin to memorize verses like the following:

* *Sing joyfully to the Lord, you righteous; it is fitting for the upright to praise him. (Psalm 33:1 NIV)*

* *Shout for joy to the Lord, all the earth. (Psalm 100:1 NIV)*

* *Enter his gates with thanksgiving and his courts with praise. (Psalm 100:4 NIV)*

* *Bless the Lord, O my soul, and forget not all his benefits. (Psalm 103:2 ESV)*

The praise and glorification of God doesn't exclusively spring from deep and untroubled understanding; it is in spite of—and even because of—deep and troubled circumstance.

—Joyce Rachelle

The Last Word

What did you think of the story of the crippled man at Gate Beautiful who was healed by Jesus? You saw his joyous response of praise when the thing he thought was impossible actually came to pass. But what about people who aren't healed in this lifetime? How many Christians do you know who go on praising even when healing doesn't come or when circumstances seem wholly unfair?

Nick Vujicic is an Australian-American Christian evangelist born with a rare disorder that caused him to have no arms and no legs. Perhaps you've seen him on television or in videos. He travels the globe, speaking in churches and at major evangelistic events. Nick is more than a motivational speaker; he's a lover of Jesus, someone who has dedicated his life to making known the praises of the Lord. And what a perspective!

"I have the choice to be angry at God for what I don't have, or be thankful for what I do have." These words from Nick are found in his book *Life without Limbs*. Can you imagine? He has chosen to praise in spite of all!

Praising God really is a choice, and it's one you can make no matter what you're going through. Consider that in light of this week's memory verse, Colossians 3:15: "And let the peace of God rule in your hearts (*no matter what*), to the which also ye are called (*you are called to peace in all circumstances*) in one body; and be ye thankful (*just as Nick is thankful despite seemingly unfair circumstances*)."

Week 5: DAY SIX
PEACE WHEN YOU'RE UNSURE

The entire validity of the Gospel rests on this remarkable story from Mark 16:1–8 (NIV):

> *When the Sabbath was over, Mary Magdalene,*
> *Mary the mother of James, and Salome bought spices*
> *so that they might go to anoint Jesus' body. Very early*
> *on the first day of the week, just after sunrise, they were*
> *on their way to the tomb and they asked each*
> *other, "Who will roll the stone away from*
> *the entrance of the tomb?"*

> *But when they looked up, they saw that the stone, which*
> *was very large, had been rolled away. As they entered*
> *the tomb, they saw a young man dressed in a white*
> *robe sitting on the right side, and they were alarmed.*

> *"Don't be alarmed," he said. "You are looking for Jesus*
> *the Nazarene, who was crucified. He has risen! He is*
> *not here. See the place where they laid him. But go,*
> *tell his disciples and Peter, 'He is going ahead of you*
> *into Galilee. There you will see him, just as he told you.' "*

> *Trembling and bewildered, the women went out*
> *and fled from the tomb. They said nothing to*
> *anyone, because they were afraid.*

Picture these three women as they arrived at the tomb to anoint the body of their deceased Savior and friend. Surely confusion, fear, and disbelief must have overwhelmed them as they looked at the place where the body had been laid. Had He been stolen? Or was the story Jesus had told them about rising again actually true?

Maybe you've been in a place where you're hopeful but shaken and unsure. You want to believe the best, but you're almost afraid to. Instead, your mind begins to conjure up all sorts of reasons why you might end up disappointed.

These women were not disappointed! Jesus really had been raised from the dead, just as He said. And you won't be disappointed, either. Even if the circumstances in front of you don't pan out exactly as you had hoped, you can still place your trust in God and be assured of His love for you. The Word of God is filled with these assurances, and by now you've leaned on scripture after scripture stating that fact.

So, if you're feeling confused today, don't give in to fear. Instead, lean on the verse you've memorized this week from Colossians 3:15: "And let the peace of God rule in your hearts (*even if you're feeling unsure*), to the which also ye are called (*to trust and be peaceful*) in one body; and be ye thankful (*knowing that His great love for you will bring only the best*)."

Trust in the LORD with all your heart, and do not lean on your own understanding. In all your ways acknowledge him, and he will make straight your paths.
PROVERBS 3:5–6 ESV

The Blank Page

A strawberry doesn't begin its journey as a large, ripe, luscious piece of fruit. It starts as a tiny white bud on a vine. When it emerges into the sunlight for the very first time, you would be hard-pressed to call it fruit at all. . .but it is! All of the potential for a yummy snack is found in that tiny little bud.

It's time to look at your scripture memory work the same way. You started out with only a tight little bud of faith. But consider Hebrews 4:12 (NIV), which says, "For the word of God is alive and active. Sharper than any double-edged sword, it penetrates even to dividing soul and spirit, joints and marrow; it judges the thoughts and attitudes of the heart."

Spending time in His Word has caused the fruit of the Spirit to spring to life inside of you. You're beginning to produce real and lasting fruit as the Word is buried deep in your heart. It springs to life every time you need a reminder or a boost of faith.

The beautiful thing about the Word of God is that it has stood the test of time. Consider the fact that hundreds of years ago, men and women put their faith and trust in the very same words you're memorizing today, though perhaps in a different version or language. For centuries, the Bible has brought hope, peace, and joy to all who take the time to read and absorb it. And you'll pass on that love for the Word to your future generations too, as they catch hold of your zeal.

The Last Word

There's a lovely story behind the old hymn "Come Thou Fount." The author, Robert Robinson, was unruly as a child. His mischief didn't stop as he aged. In fact, he grew even rowdier, turning to gambling, drinking, and carousing.

When Robert was twenty, he and his friends made a life-altering decision to go to an evangelistic meeting one night. There, they planned to heckle the preacher, a man named George Whitfield. But God had other plans! As he sat in the room and listened, Robert was overwhelmed by the presence of God and knew he must give his heart to Him.

Can you imagine all the feelings going through him that night? Like the women in the tomb, he must have gone through waves of shock, confusion, and disbelief as God began to warm his heart. Could it be true after all?

Like that tiny strawberry bud on the vine, Robert's fate was sealed. He would belong to God from that day forth and would begin to produce fruit for the kingdom.

Two years later, Robert wrote the song "Come Thou Fount," a memoir of sorts. The lyrics rang out as a testament that God could take anyone—even a lost young man like him—and turn his life around for good. He can do the same for you. Today, lay down any feelings of confusion and come to Him, fully confident of His love for you.

Oh, to grace how great a debtor
Daily I'm constrained to be
Let that goodness like a fetter
Bind my wandering heart to Thee
ROBERT ROBINSON, "COME THOU FOUNT," 1787

Week 5: DAY SEVEN
PEACE BECAUSE HIS LOVE IS REAL

Six times in the Gospel of John you will find direct or indirect references to "the disciple whom Jesus loved." Many scholars believe the disciple in question was John, brother of James. John was the youngest of the disciples, the son of Zebedee, and he authored several books of the New Testament.

How do you feel when you read the words "the disciple whom Jesus loved"? Does it seem odd that the Savior would single out one particular friend to be mentioned in such a way?

Whether we like to admit it publicly, there's usually "that one" friend or family member whom we are overly fond of. And while we would be hard-pressed to say, "I love that one most," we might secretly admit that they bring us the greatest joy.

Perhaps this was the case with John. Regardless, Jesus showed great affection for him and made known to us, the readers of the Gospels, that He had a special connection to this young man.

When you are loved—as John was loved—it can boost your morale, your courage, and the way you see yourself. That knowledge, that certainty, can also bring great peace of mind in times of turmoil. Knowing you are intimately loved means you'll never be alone. When you're resting secure in the love of the Lord, you can say with full assurance that the peace of God is ruling in your heart and that you are truly thankful for the love, grace, and mercy He has bestowed upon you.

Consider the opening words of poet Elizabeth Barrett Browning's Sonnet 43:

How do I love thee? Let me count the ways.
I love thee to the depth and breadth and height
My soul can reach, when feeling out of sight
For the ends of being and ideal grace.

Though she's speaking of romantic love, you can still see the depth, the height, the width of love expressed in her words. That's exactly how God loves you, His child! Don't believe it? Check out this passage from Ephesians 3:17–19 (NIV):

I pray that you, being rooted and established in love,
may have power, together with all the Lord's holy
people, to grasp how wide and long and high and
deep is the love of Christ, and to know this love that
surpasses knowledge—that you may be filled
to the measure of all the fullness of God.

That kind of love changes you. It leaves you different than before. Today, if you're feeling unloved, turn to the Word of God. Search for the love scriptures. Track down verses to convince yourself that the Creator of all cherishes you, His precious child.

"Greater love has no one than this,
that someone lay down his life for his friends."
JOHN 15:13 ESV

☙ The Blank Page ❧

If you've ever planted a garden, you probably know what a "volunteer" is. It's a random plant that pops up in the middle of your field of its own accord—one that was sown by an animal or blown in on the wind. Volunteers are surprises. You might have a daffodil in the middle of a watermelon patch or a cucumber in a row of lettuce heads. Surprise!

Surprises are nice, aren't they? And they're fun—a lovely reminder that some of life's blessings come without working for them.

God has filled His Word with lovely volunteers, verses that pop up and surprise you. And when you've taken the time to plant His Word in your heart, earlier crops (memory work from when you were a child, for instance) can suddenly pop up. Maybe you think of an old song you sang in Sunday school or a verse you memorized as a toddler, and those things have application for what you're going through today.

God loves to delight you, His child. Why? Because He loves you! As much as He adored John the apostle, the Lord delights in you. That's why He "volunteered" Himself on the cross. He planted Himself among an unusual crop (human beings) and sprang to life just when we needed Him most.

We should be astonished at the goodness of God,
stunned that He should bother to call us by name,
our mouths wide open at His love, bewildered that
at this very moment we are standing on holy ground.
—BRENNAN MANNING, *THE RAGAMUFFIN GOSPEL*

The Last Word

Perhaps you've read *The Practice of the Presence of God*, a book of conversations with Brother Lawrence, a seventeenth-century lay brother in a Carmelite monastery in Paris. In this beautiful book, Lawrence expresses the great intimacy and love he shared with the Lord. The love of God transformed his thinking and every moment of his life. And his story has been transforming lives ever since.

Take a look at this quote from the book:

> *The King, full of mercy and goodness, very far from chastising me, embraces me with love, makes me eat at His table, serves me with His own hands, gives me the key of His treasures; He converses and delights Himself with me incessantly, in a thousand and a thousand ways, and treats me in all respects as His favorite. It is thus I consider myself from time to time in His holy presence.*

Wow! As you read those words, perhaps you think of Lawrence, seated next to Jesus, sharing a meal. Or maybe you think of the apostle John, sitting near the Savior at the Last Supper, drinking in His every word.

Pause for a moment and think of that quote as it applies to your life! When you can picture yourself seated at the table with the King of kings, when you see only adoration pouring from His eyes as He gazes into your face, you should be flooded with peace and joy. He's given you all you could possibly need, friend, because He has given you His very life.

Week Six:

CALLED TO BE A PEACEMAKER

*Blessed are the peacemakers:
for they shall be called
the children of God.*

Matthew 5:9

Week 6: DAY ONE

PEACE WHEN YOU'RE CALLED TO A BIGGER PLAN

Queen Esther probably didn't grow up thinking she would be a queen. No doubt she saw herself as an ordinary girl, certainly not one married to a Persian king who would persecute her people, the Jews. But God had a special plan for her life, a very big plan that would save her people from destruction.

For a while, Esther hid her faith from her husband. She did this at the bidding of her cousin Mordecai. But there came a day when she could hide no longer. An evil man in the kingdom, Prime Minister Haman, insisted that everyone bow down to him. Mordecai refused to bow down, which made Haman so angry that he asked the king to murder all of the Jews.

Mordecai instructed Esther to approach the king on behalf of the Jews. This was risky business! One didn't just show up in the throne room and say, "Hey, I need a word with you." Such a visit required an invitation. But Mordecai emboldened Esther with these words: "For if you remain silent at this time, relief and deliverance for the Jews will arise from another place, but you and your father's family will perish. And who knows but that you have come to your royal position for such a time as this?" (Esther 4:14 NIV).

No pressure, right?

As you look at this week's memory verse, "Blessed are the peacemakers: for they shall be called the children of God" (Matthew 5:9), remember that there's a difference between being a peace*keeper* and a peace*maker*. Esther could have *kept* the peace in her own home by keeping her mouth shut, but God wanted to use her to *make* the peace for an entire community of people.

Esther fasted, prayed, and squared her shoulders as she marched into the throne room. Because of her bravery (and a few twists and turns in the story), the Jews were saved and Haman lost his life.

Whew! God had mighty big plans for Esther, and no doubt her knees were knocking. But her cousin's words gave her the peace and the courage to move forward, and her people were spared as a result of her bravery.

The Lord is calling you to big things too—some so big that your knees might knock and your hands might tremble. But, like Esther, He's called you "for such a time as this." And when you have that assurance—when you know in your knower that God is really behind it—then an inexplicable peace floods your soul.

What is God calling you to right here, right now? Square those shoulders and step out! Be a peacemaker, willing to take big risks for big rewards.

Since we have such a hope, we are very bold.
2 CORINTHIANS 3:12 ESV

The Blank Page

Oftentimes, a gardener will transfer a plant from one growing space to another. This is known as *transplanting*. Like Esther, these plants are often called to bigger things and require more space to spread out and grow.

When you spend time memorizing the Word of God, you're transplanting it into your heart. You're giving it access (full rein) to do whatever work the Lord has intended.

Take a look at these words from transplant surgeon Dr. Christiaan Barnard: "It is infinitely better to transplant a heart than to bury it to be devoured by worms." Of course, he was talking about the physical heart. A deceased person, buried six feet under, has no need for his heart. But think of the life it can bring to another person if transplanted!

Now think about those words in light of your journey through the Bible. Isn't it better to let the words in that Great Book settle deep in your heart than to allow them to die on a dusty shelf? Aren't they more potent, more invigorating, more life-changing when you transplant them into your heart, your mind, and your lips? When you do that, the Holy Spirit transforms and renews you in much the same way the recipient of that physical heart is transformed and renewed. You are forever changed.

Oh, the power of the Word of God! Don't let a day go by without planting it deep.

The Last Word

"The ultimate measure of a man is not where he stands in moments of comfort and convenience, but where he stands at times of challenge and controversy." These words were spoken by Rev. Martin Luther King Jr. In many ways, his story parallels Esther's. He was born "for such a time as this," to stand up for social injustice and to do all he could to save his people.

Martin was a pastor who spoke out against racial injustice in the 1960s, a time when it was not popular to do so. But he conveyed his message in a manner that allowed love and peace to pave the way. Great strides were made in the civil rights movement at his leading, and he paid the ultimate price for his bravery when his life was taken at the age of thirty-nine. He has gone down in history as one of America's bravest men.

Perhaps God won't call you to stand in front of the masses and make public proclamations, but He has placed a special call on your life, one that is meant to draw people to Him. Remember, responding to God's call with bravery will always lead to freedom in Him.

And when this happens, when we allow freedom to ring, when we let it ring from every village and hamlet, from every state and every city, we will be able to speed up that day when all of God's children, black men and white men, Jews and Gentiles, Protestants and Catholics, will be able to join hands and sing in the words of the old Negro spiritual, "Free at last! Free at last! Thank God almighty, we're free at last!"

—MARTIN LUTHER KING JR.

Week 6: DAY TWO
PEACE FOR THE HARVEST SEASON

After Jesus died and was resurrected, He ascended into heaven, which must have left His disciples very perplexed. First, He was with them (ministering/preaching), then He wasn't (after He died on the cross), then He was (when the tomb was found empty), and then He wasn't (when He ascended). But Jesus promised them that if they would wait in one accord, He would send a Helper, the Holy Spirit, to comfort and to guide. Little did they know the Holy Spirit would also give them the power to do one more thing—witness!

On the day of Pentecost, 120 people were gathered in the upper room. Suddenly, a sound like the rushing of a violent wind swept through the place, and tongues of fire appeared and rested on them. They were all filled with the Holy Spirit and began to speak with other tongues, and the Spirit enabled them (Acts 2:2–4, paraphrased).

Energized with amazing boldness, Peter addressed a large crowd that gathered. No doubt you've heard his words from Acts 2:38–41 (NIV):

> Peter replied, "Repent and be baptized, every one of you, in the name of Jesus Christ for the forgiveness of your sins. And you will receive the gift of the Holy Spirit. The promise is for you and your children and for all who are far off—for all whom the Lord our God will call."
>
> With many other words he warned them; and he

pleaded with them, "Save yourselves from this corrupt
generation." Those who accepted his message
were baptized, and about three thousand
were added to their number that day.

Whoa. Think about that for a moment. Initially, 120 people were waiting in the upper room, but 3,000 were saved and filled with the Holy Spirit because the 120 did as Jesus instructed. That's a big jump in numbers! For each person waiting in the upper room, another 25 people were swept into the kingdom. (Gotta love God's version of multiplication!) Three thousand people were radically saved, set free, and filled with the supernatural peace and joy that only the Spirit of God can bring!

The Lord is still in the soul-winning business, friend, and you should be too. That's the goal of your time in the Word: to absorb it and to become a reflection of Him so that you can win others to Him. They will be drawn to you as you are drawn to Him.

Today, take some time to pray for the harvest. May many be won to the Lord because of your life, your testimony, and your time in the Word.

Then he said to his disciples, "The harvest is plentiful,
but the laborers are few; therefore pray earnestly to the
Lord of the harvest to send out laborers into his harvest."
MATTHEW 9:37–38 ESV

❧ The Blank Page ❧

Oh, that wonderful harvest! How it must thrill a farmer's soul when reaping season is upon him. To see that the fruit of his labors is finally ready to be plucked from the ground. . .what joy! All of those hours spent preparing the soil, fertilizing, tilling, digging, planting, watering, and so on. Now, the payoff!

In many ways, that's what God must feel like when the harvest for souls is ripe, when people finally make the decision to give their hearts to Him. After all of that prep work. . .finally! Ripe for the plucking!

This is one reason we should never give up on others and never stop preaching the Gospel. People might not be won in the first conversation (or even the twenty-first), but we can't give up, because eventually the field of that heart could be ripe for harvest.

Can you see now why it's so critical to receive God's Word in your heart and allow it to shape you as a peacemaker? When you truly know the Word, when you've allowed it to transform your life, people see the changes in you. And change is irresistible to a person who also needs to change, even if he or she won't acknowledge it. Ultimately, people want true and lasting peace.

You are a soul winner for the kingdom of God, so hold tight to the Word of truth and be ready in season and out. Before long, you'll see a true harvest of souls if you don't give up.

❧ The Last Word ❧

Mention the name of Billy Graham in almost any country in the world, and people will immediately know who you're talking about. This remarkable man of God was a soul winner, passionate for the cause of winning men and women to the Lord. He was also a peacemaker who traveled with and ministered to presidents and kings.

Like the farmer reaping a harvest, Billy Graham won souls by the thousands. Like Esther, he was born "for such a time as this," when large crusades were welcomed and well-attended. People of every race, ethnicity, age, and gender would cram together in stadiums just to hear him preach the Word of God.

And boy, did he ever have the Word in him! Billy Graham was so saturated in the Word that it literally flowed from him like water, which was obvious while watching him preach. He loved the calling God placed on his life. Check out what he had to say about the thrill of it all: "I still enjoy watching a batter successfully cross home plate, but nothing thrills me more than seeing the Holy Spirit at work in hearts as the Gospel is carried into stadiums, across the airwaves, and around the world."

During harvest seasons, there will always be those ready and willing to preach the Gospel. Hopefully, you are one of them! And remember, if you can't preach with your lips, use your life to preach.

A return to the Bible would also give inner peace and security that people are desperately looking for. How wonderful to hear the words of Christ: "My peace I give to you" (John 14:27).
—Billy Graham, address to the 150th Annual Meeting of The American Bible Society

Week 6: DAY THREE
PEACE WHEN HOT-BUTTON TOPICS ARISE

You've been there. Things are going along great in your friend group or family gathering. Then someone brings up a hot-button topic. Oh no! Peace flies out the window. Tempers rise. Folks get angry. One storms out. Another insists she's never speaking to the others again.

Oh, brother. Everything about these responses is wrong, wouldn't you say? Jesus wants us to walk in love and understanding with each other, not put up walls and storm away.

You might think hot-button topics are a twenty-first-century problem, but think again! Jesus' brother James dealt with a serious one. He was an early church leader who addressed a topic that was not only "hot" but extra sensitive as well. Circumcision.

Yep, he went there. "Do new believers (Gentiles) need to be circumcised in order to become Christians?" Under the old law, the act of circumcision was demanded; but if salvation came by grace, why put someone through that unnecessarily?

James stood up and addressed the topic once and for all, deciding that Gentiles should not have to agree to circumcision. The decision was also made that they would not have to follow the customs found in the law. A compromise was struck: the Gentiles would abstain from a few select foods and would refrain from sexual immorality.

Whew! Compromise! Suddenly, the hot-button topic was diffused as the apostles (*gasp!*) came into agreement.

The same thing is possible today. If friends approach these

difficult topics with grace and peace leading the way, they can walk away without feeling they've been attacked. There's a difference between being bold and being foolish. A foolish person blasts others with his sometimes overly strong opinion, taking no account of how he's coming across. A bold believer will speak truth with confidence but brimming with self-control and love.

Consider this quote from Christian leader Pat Robertson: "Jesus Christ is a prince of peace. He told us to live in peace. He told us to love our enemies. He told us to do good to them that spitefully use us."

When you choose to handle hard topics this way, God is honored and feelings are spared. Does this mean you back away from biblical truth? Absolutely not. But make your case kindly, using words that Jesus would use if He happened to be leading the conversation.

He *is* leading the conversation, by the way. Using the power of His Spirit, He speaks through you. That's why it's important to know what the Bible says about relevant, hot-button topics. When you're well-versed, you can open your mouth and speak truth in love. . .with authority.

Then we will no longer be infants, tossed back and forth by the waves, and blown here and there by every wind of teaching and by the cunning and craftiness of people in their deceitful scheming. Instead, speaking the truth in love, we will grow to become in every respect the mature body of him who is the head, that is, Christ. From him the whole body, joined and held together by every supporting ligament, grows and builds itself up in love, as each part does its work.
EPHESIANS 4:14–16 NIV

The Blank Page

When hot-button topics come up in a conversation, the peacekeepers usually get up and start pacing. They just want it to stop, for tempers to cool. Peacemakers, especially those who feel driven by the Spirit to speak truth, might keep going but do so in love, not anger. This is why it's so good to have the Word of God planted deep in your heart. In the very middle of a hot-button moment, you can analyze the situation from that point of view.

When gentle truth should be spoken, go ahead and speak it; don't hide it. Your opinion might not be popular, but it can be presented in love. And if you keep your arms wide open, loving those who feel differently, no one can accuse you of putting up walls.

In some ways, you're like a bee pollinating a flower. You're gently taking nectar from the Word of God and planting it in the next flower (the person you're sharing with). Your intent is not to damage or destroy that flower in any way; rather, you fertilize it so that it might grow.

Perhaps Catholic bishop Francis de Sales said it best: "The bee collects honey from flowers in such a way as to do the least damage or destruction to them, and he leaves them whole, undamaged and fresh, just as he found them."

The process should be gentle and always with the other person in mind. That's how love leads the way, and that's how peace wins.

The Last Word

Perhaps you already know the story of Dietrich Bonhoeffer (1906–1945). You might expect him to be genteel and kind because he was a Lutheran pastor, but he lived during Hitler's era of Nazism, which deeply contradicted his faith. So, he had a choice to make—speak the truth and risk all or keep his mouth shut.

Bonhoeffer decided to be bold. He acted and used his platform for good. He spoke truth, mincing no words: "We are not to simply bandage the wounds of victims beneath the wheels of injustice, we are to drive a spoke into the wheel itself."

The center of German Protestant resistance to the Nazi regime was the "confessing church," which wasn't recognized by the state, of which Bonhoeffer became lead spokesman. Can you imagine the opposition he must have faced as he took a stand against death and destruction?

Perhaps his life message was best summed up in these words: "Silence in the face of evil is itself evil: God will not hold us guiltless. Not to speak is to speak. Not to act is to act."

Bonhoeffer paid a heavy price for speaking up. He was arrested and later executed in a concentration camp. But his memory lives on, and his role as a peacemaker is undeniable. If Christians hadn't taken a stand, where would the country be today?

Bonhoeffer played a critical role in the story. And he found peace in speaking truth, as is evidenced in his words: "One act of obedience is better than one hundred sermons."

Week 6: DAY FOUR
PEACE WHEN SHOOTING FOR PERFECTION

No doubt you've heard about her. You might have even met her—in the neighborhood, at the school, on social media. The Proverbs 31 woman. She's that gal who's practically perfect in every way. She cooks, cleans, is kind to others, has the perfect husband, lives in a great home, even her children adore her and sing her praises. She's crafty, she's perky, she's pretty, she's well put together.

You, on the other hand? You're a hot mess. Between your job, kids, housework, carpooling, church, and so on, you can barely get your act together. There are dirty dishes in the sink, your husband can't find a clean shirt, and the kids are complaining that the dog ate their shoes. You glance in the mirror and realize you forgot to brush your hair today. Lovely.

So, how do you obtain peace when you're striving to be practically perfect in every way? Is that even possible? Or, do you just give up and say, "Nope, ain't gonna go there. I'll be disappointed if I try."

Here's the deal: you'll never be perfect in this lifetime, but that doesn't mean you can't shoot high. As the old adage by Norman Vincent Peale goes: "Shoot for the moon. Even if you miss, you'll land among the stars." Aiming for perfection is good because it gives you a lofty target, just as aiming for the dot in the center of a dartboard gives you something to aim for. But no one expects that dart to land on the dot every time.

So, what do you suppose Jesus meant in Matthew 5:48 (ESV) when He said, "You therefore must be perfect, as your heavenly

Father is perfect"? If we're never going to fully measure up, why would He say that?

He's the dot on the dartboard. He's the Proverbs 31 picture of perfection, only ten thousand times more so. He wants you to shoot high, to aim at the moon, as it were. If you check out the very next verse (Matthew 6:1 ESV), you'll see that He also says, "Beware of practicing your righteousness before other people in order to be seen by them, for then you will have no reward from your Father who is in heaven." Were these two thoughts meant to go together, perhaps? Sometimes those modern Proverbs 31 gals love to paint pretty pictures on social media, carrying on about their perfect lives; but if you really scratch the surface, you often find that they're anything but perfect.

Shoot high. You might not hit the mark, but at least you're trying. The key is to be content wherever you land. Learn to make peace with yourself about your own expectations so that you're not always disappointed.

Not that I have already obtained this or am already perfect, but I press on to make it my own, because Christ Jesus has made me his own.
PHILIPPIANS 3:12 ESV

The Blank Page

There's a new movement in the food community where consumers are being asked not to reject imperfect fruits and vegetables. In fact, they're encouraged to buy them despite their bumps and wrinkles.

Maybe you balk at that idea. You want your tomatoes to be without spot or blemish. You love your bell peppers to be beautifully rounded. You're very finicky about the lack of speckles on your bananas.

Think of this situation from a farmer's perspective. Say he's producing a field of cucumbers. Maybe 60 percent of them are perfect, but the rest? Not so much. They're like you, staring in the mirror, comparing yourself to the Proverbs 31 woman. Bumps. Wrinkles. Warts. Flaws. What does he do with that additional 40 percent that he can't sell to the supermarkets or vegetable stands? Unless someone intervenes, he tosses it in the rubbish bin or feeds it to the pigs.

It's time to recognize the fact that the Farmer (Jesus) sees you as perfect! When He looks at you, He sees you through His own righteousness. You're spotless! White as snow! As we read in 2 Corinthians 5:17 (ESV): "Therefore, if anyone is in Christ, he is a new creation. The old has passed away; behold, the new has come." That's how you are viewed by your heavenly Father, and it's time you started seeing yourself that way! Make peace with Him, and you can make peace with yourself. It really is that simple.

❧ The Last Word ❧

When you hear the name Mother Teresa, what images come to mind? Do you see a gorgeous woman, dressed to the nines, with a perfect house and shoes? Do you see someone singing her own praises and talking about how ideal her life is? Do you see a woman making a big splash about her latest vacation or expensive purchases?

No, Mother Teresa, who worked with orphans in Calcutta, India, was anything but that. She drew close to the people around her, wearing no makeup, dressing humbly, and not styling her hair. If you put her picture on social media, people would be more apt to stare than to say, "Wow, what a gal!"

And yet, what a gal she was! Teresa made peace with Jesus early in her life and dedicated her life to Him. She made peace with herself when she accepted the call to minister to the poor in India. And because of these decisions, she became one of the most beautiful women ever to walk the planet. She loved deeply, accomplished great things, and shared the love of Jesus with the masses.

Today, choose to be like Teresa. As you memorize this week's verse, remind yourself that God's calling on your life was hand-picked for you, and making peace with Him will ensure a lifetime of beauty.

> *Let us always meet each other with a smile,*
> *for the smile is the beginning of love.*
> —MOTHER TERESA

Week 6: DAY FIVE
PEACE TO FACE THE REFLECTION IN THE MIRROR

God rejected Saul as king over Israel, and it was up to Samuel the prophet to find the next king. The Lord instructed him to choose from among the sons of Jesse. No worries there; Jesse had plenty of fine, strapping boys.

One by one, the young men passed before Samuel, but each time, he felt a check in his spirit: "Nope, that's not the one." When the parade of sons passed by, Samuel asked Jesse, "Is that it? Is that all you have?"

There was one more—young David, the shepherd boy. But he was busy tending to the sheep. The story picks up in 1 Samuel 16:11–13 (NIV):

> Samuel said, "Send for him;
> we will not sit down until he arrives."

> So he [Jesse] sent for him [David] and had him
> brought in. He was glowing with health and had
> a fine appearance and handsome features.

> Then the LORD said,
> "Rise and anoint him; this is the one."

> So Samuel took the horn of oil and anointed him in
> the presence of his brothers, and from that day on
> the Spirit of the LORD came powerfully upon
> David. Samuel then went to Ramah.

It's almost comical at times, how we make our choices based

on outward appearance, isn't it? We pick our favorite quarterbacks based on their size, we choose pageant winners based on their beauty and physique, and sometimes we even pick our friends because we think they're a good fit appearance-wise.

How God must laugh! He doesn't care about outward appearance, so why do we?

That's a legitimate question, by the way. Why do you care so much about your own outward appearance? Why are you troubled by that double chin or those wrinkles? Why so bummed about the cellulite or long nose? You judge yourself so harshly at times, and you shouldn't.

Society cares about such things, but God never has, and neither should you. Sure, you need to put your best foot forward and learn to dress the body He's given you. But when you cross that invisible line in the sand (you know the one) and start to care too much about the physical, things can get wonky. You can give in to despair or run toward the plastic surgeon's office; either way, things won't end well.

Or. . .you can come to Jesus with your concerns about your appearance. He will help you come to peace with who you are and what you look like. With His help, you won't stare in the mirror, disgusted by what you see staring back. You were created in the image of God, after all, and He's not repulsed by you. He sees His beautiful child, radiant and filled with His Spirit!

Today, ask for His eyes to see yourself the way He does. And make peace—lasting peace—with the reflection in the mirror. Celebrate it!

"Stop judging by mere appearances,
but instead judge correctly."
JOHN 7:24 NIV

The Blank Page

Some people are so twisted up inside about how they look that it affects their witness. They're afraid to stand in front of a Bible study group and give a testimony, because someone might judge their chubby thighs or graying hair. Instead, they slink into the background and let someone else do the talking.

God created you to share your story. Your words give life to the body, and those words aren't limited or even affected by appearance! They have the power to transform lives!

Revelation 12:11 says: "And they overcame him by the blood of the Lamb, and by the word of their testimony; and they loved not their lives unto the death."

It's your story, your testimony, that wins people to Him! Consider this quote from poet Anthony Liccione: "It's not the appearance that makes a man, it's the man that makes an appearance."

Make an appearance, friend. Show up. Go there. If you've been letting anything hold you back from sharing your story, let it go! Don't worry about what they're thinking. They won't be focused on your outward appearance as you're speaking, anyway. They'll be too busy hanging on your every word as you share the remarkable work Christ has done in your heart.

❦ The Last Word ❦

At first glance, you might not recognize the name Dave Roever. But if you saw a picture, you would know immediately that he must have an extraordinary story. Dave grew up in a Christian home in Texas. He was drafted during the Vietnam War and joined the navy. Eight months to the day into his tour of duty, something horrific happened. A phosphorus grenade he was poised to throw exploded in his hand. Dave was burned beyond recognition.

It took fourteen months in the hospital and numerous surgeries, but Dave survived. His face and body still carry the scars of his ordeal, but those who know him will tell you that's not what people see.

If you go to a service to hear Dave speak, you hear his remarkable testimony and his overwhelming love for the Savior. He exudes peace, joy, and hope. He also has a terrific sense of humor.

While many would have grown bitter, Dave has only grown better. And those scars—ugly as they might have seemed to him in the early months—have become his testimony. They have opened doors for him to speak to multitudes, including world leaders.

You can grow better too. No matter what you've faced, no matter how it has affected you physically, you still have the potential for your story to change the world. Hold tight to the promises found in the Word, and lean on this week's memory verse. Make peace with your body, and then allow God to use you to reach others.

Week 6: DAY SIX
PEACE BECAUSE HE TORE THE VEIL

Several things happened simultaneously when Jesus died on the cross. Of course, the most significant event and the thing for which we're ultimately most thankful is that He took our sins with Him to the grave. But other things happened in the moment Jesus died. He passed away at 3:00 p.m., which was the exact time the Jews killed the Passover lamb in the temple. Talk about timely and symbolic! He was our sacrificial lamb, laying down His life for us.

Also, at the moment of His death, the veil in the temple was torn in two. It ripped from the top all the way down to the ground below. Think about that for a moment. No one used scissors or a knife. The curtain separating the Holy of Holies (the most holy place, where ordinary people were not allowed to go) from the outer courts was gone. Everyday people now had full access to God in the inner sanctum.

"For he himself is our peace, who has made the two groups one and has destroyed the barrier, the dividing wall of hostility" (Ephesians 2:14 NIV). We have been granted access to God through Christ's death!

At that same moment, an earthquake hit and, according to Matthew 27:51–52, many ancient prophets came alive again. Can we just stop right there? Dead people came back to life at the very moment Jesus gave His life for us. Is there any clearer sign that His death was actually meant to bring life? The cross changes everything!

At the cross, at the cross where I first saw the light,
And the burden of my heart rolled away,
It was there by faith I received my sight,
And now I am happy all the day!
—Isaac Watts, "At the Cross"

When you dig into the Word of God and memorize sections of it, hidden gems like these can spring forth! You can learn vast secrets and uncover many mysteries. Best of all, you can see how the stories buried in those pages aren't meant to be simple stories at all but, rather, instruments to bring lasting change in your heart, your life, and the circumstances swirling around you.

That's the beauty of the torn veil, friend. You have access to God. You have full access to His words, His thoughts, His joy, His peace, His eternal life. You are ushered in, and all because of what Jesus did for you on the cross.

At that moment the curtain of the temple was torn in two
from top to bottom. The earth shook, the rocks split and the
tombs broke open. The bodies of many holy people who had
died were raised to life. They came out of the tombs after
Jesus' resurrection and went into the holy city
and appeared to many people.
Matthew 27:51–53 NIV

The Blank Page

When you look at a deceased person, you don't usually think about life. Rather, you grieve the death and feel the loss with great sadness. But when you gaze at the cross of Christ, you're struck by a different idea: the cross symbolizes new life, new hope, and new joys.

The thirtieth chapter of Deuteronomy tells us that we're given a choice between life and death and that we should "choose this day whom we will serve." It's fascinating to think that the God of the universe would give us a choice! But He never forces people to follow Him, only hopes they will see His sacrifice and be drawn to Him.

Today, if you haven't made peace with the King of the universe, if you haven't asked Jesus Christ to come into your heart and be the Lord of all, take the time to do so. Accepting His work on the cross and applying it to your life will change everything! Only when you make peace with God can you make peace with yourself and others around you.

Remember, Jesus sprang forth from the tomb—much as that little plant springs forth from the garden. The evidence of life was visible for all to see! The same will be true in your heart too! People will notice once you've been reborn. The changes they see in you will be undeniable, and they will want to experience what you've been through as well.

Dig into the Word of God and look up all the verses about the cross of Christ. You will be astounded at how many times it shows up across the pages. Adding the cross to any story changes it dramatically. Today, if you haven't already done so, allow it to change yours.

❧ The Last Word ❧

Think about the people in your world—family members, friends, coworkers, church buddies, pastors, and so on. Among those folks, how many had what you might call a "radical" conversion to Christ? Perhaps you know someone who was into crime or drugs or alcohol. Then they had an encounter with Jesus that changed everything.

Over the course of time, there have been hundreds of thousands of newsworthy conversions, stories of people being miraculously saved. Of course, these radical conversions were nothing new to Christendom. One of the first documented conversion stories was that of the apostle Paul in the book of Acts. Paul (formerly Saul) was putting Christians to death, so it's difficult to believe that he would end up joining their ranks. But that is exactly what happened on the road to Damascus one day.

> *As he neared Damascus on his journey, suddenly a light from heaven flashed around him. He fell to the ground and heard a voice say to him, "Saul, Saul, why do you persecute me?"*
>
> *"Who are you, Lord?" Saul asked.*
>
> *"I am Jesus, whom you are persecuting,"*
> *he replied. "Now get up and go into the city, and you will be told what you must do."*
>
> ACTS 9:3–6 NIV

Suffice it to say, God knows how to get our attention. He shook Paul's world in order to change his mind, and He will do no less for those you are praying for. Don't give up! Jesus—the true Peacemaker—is willing to go to any lengths to change the hearts of those He loves.

Week 6: DAY SEVEN
PEACE IN THE BODY OF CHRIST

How will we win the world for Jesus? How will the church make the kind of impact that will bring lasting peace and hope to the lost? The answer: when peace reigns inside the body of Christ.

People are people. Individuals are individuals. God never meant for us to be cookie cutters of one another. But if we would all put our differences aside and focus on Jesus first, loving others second, and ourselves last, what a difference we could make!

Over the past six weeks, you've taken a close look at what the Bible has to say about peace. You've memorized scriptures to help with your personal journey, and you've examined the stories of men and women in biblical times and throughout history who've allowed peace to reign in their hearts too. You see that it is possible as long as the Word is planted deep within your heart.

So, what can you do to make sure the church is strong? How can you make a difference? Start by laying down any quarrels and disputes. Forgive those who have hurt you. Make up your mind to walk in unity despite your disagreements. If the early Christians could do it, you can too.

Bible study teacher Elizabeth George said, "Our conduct is an advertisement for or against Jesus Christ. That's why unity in the body of Christ is so important." She's right! The world is watching the church to see if we're really who we say we are. If there's no peace inside the walls of the church, do you think a lost world is going to want what we say we have?

So, how do we get there? How do we get past the things we

can't seem to agree on? The answer is found in 1 Peter 3:8 (ESV): "Finally, all of you, have unity of mind, sympathy, brotherly love, a tender heart, and a humble mind." It all begins with humility. If someone asks you, "How do I fix any broken relationship and bring lasting peace?" start with the words "Humble yourself."

God said it too. In 2 Chronicles 7:14 (NIV), He said, "If my people, who are called by my name, will humble themselves and pray and seek my face and turn from their wicked ways, then I will hear from heaven, and I will forgive their sin and will heal their land." It starts with humility, and each person must do his or her part.

Are there any rifts in your relationships with fellow believers? Start there. Humble yourself. Make things right. Then live a life that encourages others to walk in humility. If every believer would live this way, peace would reign in every church, and together—fully unified—we would reach the world with the Gospel.

Finally, brothers, rejoice. Aim for restoration, comfort one another, agree with one another, live in peace; and the God of love and peace will be with you.

2 CORINTHIANS 13:11 ESV

The Blank Page

A vegetable garden is a beautiful sight—all of those colors, one after the other, in lovely rows. Tomatoes, carrots, zucchini, onions, and cucumbers all live together in perfect harmony, never arguing, bickering, or picking fights.

Modern planters, especially those with rooftop gardens or small spaces, are also merging vegetables and flowers. Petunias grow alongside spicy peppers. Bulky heads of lettuce comingle with daffodils. Eggplants nestle into spaces beside rose bushes. Some gardeners will even "tuck" vegetables into gardens with existing flowers, taking advantage of every space. Can you imagine how colorful those garden spaces are? They dwell in perfect harmony.

Isn't this a picture of what the body of Christ should look like? God intended for us to comingle, to cohabitate. Red and yellow, black and white, we are all precious in the sight of our heavenly Father. And harmony is possible, even when we're vastly different in personality, as long as we're submitted to His authority in our lives.

The longer you spend in the Word, the more you see how important this principle is for spiritual growth. If you, as an individual, can come to fullness of Christ and make peace with Him, He will help you make peace with others, even those vastly different from yourself.

Make this your goal, friend. May your time in the Bible drive you to a deeper relationship with Christ so that He can push you to a deeper relationship with others.

The Last Word

Christian apologist Ravi Zacharias spent the summer of 1971 in South Vietnam, where he had traveled for one express purpose: to evangelize US soldiers and imprisoned Vietcong members. This was just the beginning of what would turn out to be a passionate evangelistic ministry. Soul winning was key to Ravi, who traveled the globe sharing the Gospel. When he spoke with students in Moscow after the fall of the Berlin Wall, doors opened for Ravi to enter the political sphere. God then offered him multiple opportunities to speak in front of world leaders.

In his book, *The Grand Weaver*, Ravi said, "When God brings us to salvation, the most remarkable thing we see is that He transforms our hungers. He changes not just what we do but what we want to do. This is the work of the Holy Spirit within us—'for it is God who works in you to will and to act according to his good purpose' (Philippians 2:13)."

For Ravi, that hunger was for the Word of God. He studied it, absorbed it, took it to heart. Because of his countless hours in the Bible, he became a renowned scholar and apologist who impacted the world.

Maybe you'll never be a Ravi Zacharias or a Billy Graham. Maybe you won't preach from behind a pulpit or be ushered into the presence of kings. But if you give yourself over to a lifetime of learning and gleaning from the Word, you will be transformed by God's supernatural peace, and your transformation will affect the lives of everyone with whom you come into contact. So, what are you waiting for? Grab that Bible, and let's get going!

I press on toward the goal for the prize
of the upward call of God in Christ Jesus.
PHILIPPIANS 3:14 ESV

THESE THINGS I HAVE SPOKEN UNTO YOU,
THAT IN ME YE MIGHT HAVE PEACE. IN THE WORLD
YE SHALL HAVE TRIBULATION: BUT BE OF GOOD
CHEER; I HAVE OVERCOME THE WORLD.

JOHN 16:33

THE LORD WILL GIVE STRENGTH
UNTO HIS PEOPLE; THE LORD WILL
BLESS HIS PEOPLE WITH PEACE.

PSALM 29:11

Thou wilt keep him in perfect peace,
whose mind is stayed on thee:
because he trusteth in thee.

Isaiah 26:3

IF IT BE POSSIBLE, AS MUCH AS LIETH
IN YOU, LIVE PEACEABLY WITH ALL MEN.

ROMANS 12:18

AND LET THE PEACE OF GOD RULE IN YOUR HEARTS, TO THE WHICH ALSO YE ARE CALLED IN ONE BODY; AND BE YE THANKFUL.

Colossians 3:15

BLESSED ARE THE PEACEMAKERS: FOR THEY
SHALL BE CALLED THE CHILDREN OF GOD.

MATTHEW 5:9